LAS VARAS

LAS VARAS

Ritual and Ethnicity in the Ancient Andes

Howard Tsai

The University of Alabama Press Tuscaloosa

The University of Alabama Press
Tuscaloosa, Alabama 35487-0380
uapress.ua.edu

Typeface: Caslon

Cover image: Panpipe fragment (4.7 cm) found at Las Varas;
courtesy of Howard Tsai
Cover design: David Nees

Cataloging-in-Publication data is available from the Library
of Congress.
ISBN: 978-0-8173-2068-3
E-ISBN: 978-0-8173-9320-5

Contents

Illustrations

Figures

Tables

Acknowledgments

Writing a book is quite the alienating and solitary affair—nasty, brutish, and long. There are of course many moments of joy in the process, like when the author recounts those who have given him guidance, support, care, wisdom, joviality, and love. Similar to Elgar's Enigma Variations, I dedicate each chapter to a group of family, friends, and mentors, but unlike that famous musical riddle, here I reveal the names of those individuals.

The entire book is dedicated to my family. I am fortunate to have the unwavering support of my mother, father, sister, and grandparents to pursue such an unconventional study as archaeology. I am sorry to have worried them by traveling so far from home, and I thank my parents for visiting me in Peru during my fieldwork. I am very happy and blessed to have their endless love and understanding.

The interconnectedness of this book's chapters, the sinews binding data and theory, owes much to the intellectual complexity of my core group of mentors: Joyce Marcus, Bruce Mannheim, and Kent Flannery. Joyce was my dissertation advisor, and the amount of time, labor, and energy she expended solely for the advancement of my studies has always astounded me, then and now. In my doctoral thesis (2012), I promised her a "lifetime subscription to my future publications"; by now, she must have realized that that was a bum deal, but at least she will soon receive a monograph in the mail. Thank you, Joyce, for this book could not have been written without your infinite patience and mentorship.

I am indebted to Bruce Mannheim, whose knowledge of cutting-edge linguistic anthropology and semiotics theory is like a persuasive agent provocateur (but working for the good guys) inspiring me to think boldly and daringly. We shall have more theoretical parleys in Cusco over chicha and Cusqueña. I was accompanied by two important books during my eighteen-month dissertation fieldwork in Peru: Edmund Leach's *Political Systems of Highland Burma* and Kent Flannery's *The Early Mesoamerican Village*. I was incredibly fortunate, then, to have taken many classes with Kent in Michigan, for not only had I learned much from his insightful analyses and syntheses, but it was also fantastic to hear, in person, Kent's telling and retelling of the great (and not-so-great) moments in archaeology.

I believe I once told my good friends Casey Barrier, Cameron Gokee, and Alice Wright that "theory is a battle of metaphors," so I dedicate the introductory chapter to them, who I hope will enjoy evocations of tree, staircase, billiard balls, and poker in my narrative of ethnicity theory in anthropology and archaeology. To them I add a host of colleagues, mentors, and friends from my graduate school days in Ann Arbor: Henry Wright, Bob Whallon, Jeff Parsons, John O'Shea, Carla Sinopoli, Geoff Emberling, Gustavo Verdesio, Karma Cochran, Paul Duffy, Ana Jankovic, Hemanth Kadambi, Bella Muntz, Jonathan Devore, Andy Gurstelle, Tim Horlsey, Matt Gallon, Leland Davis, Ivan Cangemi, and Chelsea Fisher.

Chapter 1, which treats ethnic groups and their interaction in the *chaupi-yunga* zone, is written for my Andeanist friends not specializing in archaeology: Guillermo Salas, Sergio Huarcaya, Josh Shapero, Angelica Serna, Nick Emlen, Randall "Luigi" Hicks, and Allie Caine. I hope they can find a modicum of intellectual worth in this product sprung from an archaeologist's unrefined though artless mind.

Chapter 2 sets Las Varas in its environmental and archaeological context within the Jequetepeque Valley, and thus it is a tribute to "Team Farfán"—Robyn Cutright, Abigail Levine, Gabriela Cervantes, Jason Toohey, Hugo Ikehara, Enrique Zavaleta, César Jáuregui, and Jorge Terrones—rank-and-file archaeologists who have worked under the directorship of Carol Mackey at the Lambayeque-Chimú-Inca site of Farfán. Carol deserves credit for being the muse and mentor behind chapters 3, 4, and 5, for she taught me that most valuable of lessons in excavation, which is to always ask "why am I digging here" and "what is the question I am trying to answer." I treasure those moments when I stood next to Carol, sun-, wind-, and sand-blasted in the Peruvian desert, as she explained and discussed with me the stratigraphy or architectural feature within an excavation unit—those were halcyon days.

Chapter 3 is the result of my interactions with a special cadre of archaeologists who spent a lifetime digging on the north coast of Peru: Christopher Donnan, Luis Jaime Castillo, John Topic, Jerry Moore, and Tom Dillehay. I would also like to include Charles "Chip" Stanish, and even though he doesn't work on the north coast, readers finishing this chapter will understand my appreciation for his theoretical and methodological framework. I thank them for their kindness and generosity to a young man wanting to become an archaeologist.

Chapter 4 presents data from our excavation of residential structures, and here it is fitting that I thank the individuals who have made Peru my home away from home. I give my deepest thanks to the Bazán family of Pay Pay (Patty, Huner, Marcela, Maria, Hugo, Darlin, Ayrton, Jeraldo, and Jeyson) who took me in as a member of the clan and gave me so much warmth and joy that I never felt lonely during my one-and-a-half-year stay. Through them I was introduced to the Andean kin network: whenever I traveled between the coast, middle valley, and highlands, Señor Andrés Bazán and Señora Santos Bazán always made sure that I could find a *primo* or *compadre* in the towns or villages I was visiting. Their friendship and *cariño* shaped my understanding of exchange and interaction in the Andes; as a result, I now conceptualize *los Estados Unidos* as a "vertical archipelago" extension of Pay Pay.

In 2013, about a year after I finished my PhD, I had the wonderful opportunity to teach and live in Cusco, and there I was received with hospitality and affection by the Galiano family (Viky, Jesús, Yeshica, Carmen, Chewy, Hania, and Sunaca). I miss with great fondness my ventures with Margarita Huayhua, Amy Mortensen, and Adela Carlos into some of Cusco's most Hadean *picanterías*. Jean-Jacques Decoster has taught me more about living, surviving, and prospering in Cusco than anyone in this wide and alien world. I hope he is not working too hard on a fine Friday evening, for that is when I wish to be chatting with him, in a restaurant with the best view of the old capital, about anthropology, Andean ethnohistory, and Inca archaeology.

Excavation of the ritual structures at Las Varas, covered in chapter 5, provided some of the most exciting moments in fieldwork, so here I express my gratitude to members of the Las Varas Archaeological Project: Leonardo Murga, Luis Chuquipoma, Nicolás "Totti" Gálvez, Solsiré Cusicanqui, Maritza Bazán, Huner Bazán, Napoleón Bazán, Lorenzo Bazán, Julio León, Clemente León, José "Pachi" Palacios, Khori Newlander, and Alexi Smith. We often placed bets on what surprise the next construction stage of the Reception Platform would yield—the loser had to buy a case of beer. I could not have asked for a better team of workers.

Chapter 5 contains details of archaeological excavation and architectural reconstruction, information that would appeal to "Real Andean Archaeologists," so I proffer this chapter to Véronique Bélisle, Allison Davis, Alan Covey, Jordan Dalton, John Warner, Ed Swenson, Eisei Tsurumi, and Shinya Watanabe.

Michael Lempert and Jason De León have thrown great parties at their place in Ann Arbor, and the celebratory nature of these gatherings reminds me of the ceremonies that would have taken place in the Plazas of the Malquis, except that they desecrate rather than consecrate the ancestors. I thank Jason and Michael for having such a lovely family.

The last chapter of this book, chapter 6, was conceived during my "second life" working as a university administrator at the Center for Latin American and Caribbean Studies at the University of Michigan. Who would have guessed that office culture lends itself to thoughts of game theory? I am grateful to my colleagues and comrades at the center, Lenny Ureña, Bebete Martins, and Alexandra Stern, and also to Nataša Gruden-Alajbegović and Kelsey Szpara at the International Institute. Lenny beat me in having her book completed and published first, and I thank her for embarking with me on this dissertation-to-book expedition. I deeply appreciate the moral support I received from Lenny and Bebete, which invariably took the form of improv comedy and karaoke. Michael Prentice and Ujin Kim deserve my thanks for stimulating conversations on theory and philosophy.

I always learn interesting things from my students in the Program in International and Comparative Studies at the University of Michigan, especially those who were in my Cusco Global Course Connection. Their intelligence, perseverance, resilience, creativity, and energy are an inspiration. Wendi Schnaufer at the University of Alabama Press has been constantly helping and encouraging me to reach the finish line, and so she receives this final "thank you."

The Las Varas Archaeological Project was made possible by generous funding from the Social Science Research Council, Fulbright-Hays Program, the American Philosophical Society, the James B. Griffin Research Award from the University of Michigan Museum of Anthropology, the University of Michigan Rackham Graduate School, and the University of Michigan Department of Anthropology.

LAS VARAS

Introduction

Imagine for a moment that you are an archaeologist surveying a valley in northern Peru. Your objective is to take your team and walk over the hills and flatlands on both sides of the river, find and document extant archaeological sites, record their location with a handheld GPS, take notes and photos of artifacts and architecture (if any), and make inferences on the age, culture, and sociopolitical system of these ancient settlements.

One site you discover has pieces of painted pottery scattered on the surface. Its cemetery has funerary chambers made of stone. An hour's walk downriver you find another site, but this time, on the surface, is plain, unpainted pottery, and its cemetery has simple, unmarked tombs. Analysis shows that these two sites were contemporaries—they both date to the eleventh century AD. What was the relationship between these two communities a thousand years ago? Did they know of each other's existence? If so, did they trade, intermarry, or simply ignore each other? Why did they use different kinds of pottery, and why did they bury their dead differently?

It is not unusual for archaeologists to detect such contrasts between adjacent, contemporary sites: they often find sites or groups of sites that, despite having different artifacts, architecture, and cultural materials, date to the same time period. The opening anecdote is, in fact, based on my own experience in the field and became the genesis of an archaeological project at Las Varas in the Middle Jequetepeque Valley (Figure I.1). I first visited and took note of the site in 2005, unaware that it had been registered by Eisei Tsurumi a year earlier (Tsurumi et al. 2004). Las Varas was unique compared to neighboring sites because it had distinct types of pottery, burials, houses, and other material remains. On that first visit, I immediately recognized the site's potential for investigating ethnicity and colonization, and a few days later I decided to excavate Las Varas for my doctoral project. Excavation commenced in 2006, and throughout fieldwork I had to confront the challenge of interpreting the strange style of objects and structures

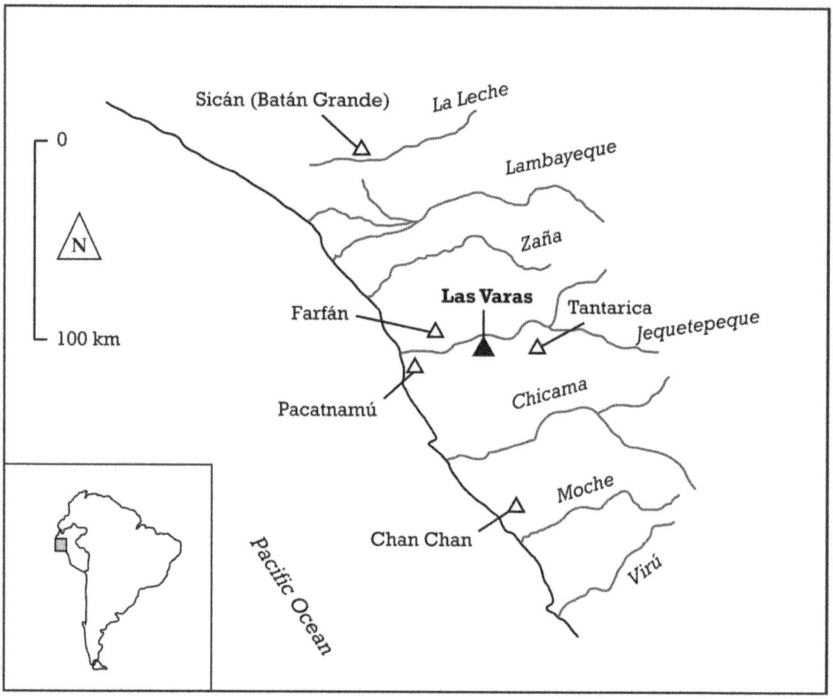

Figure I.1. Map of Peru, showing Las Varas. (Courtesy of Howard Tsai)

found at the site. Did a foreign culture or ethnic group migrate into the area and make their home at Las Varas?

An assemblage of artifacts and material remains (e.g., pottery, stone tools, houses, burials, temples) found in a particular geographical area and dating to a particular time period is known as the "archaeological culture." One archaeological culture can be distinguished from another by the style, look, or design of its objects, so that an archaeologist picking up a piece of pottery can say, "*that* is Lambayeque" or "*that* is Chimu." But even if the archaeological culture is clearly defined and easily recognizable, we cannot be sure whether it correlated with ancient social groupings; such an inference requires further investigation.

Emily Stovel (2013) cautions against equating the archaeological culture with an ethnic group in her review of studies of ethnicity in Andean archaeology. She observes that, in the context of Andean studies, the ethnic group had been linked to kin-based communities or larger political entities like the *ayllu* or *señorío*, which frequently appear in ethnohistory and ethnography. The second motif that influenced concepts of ethnicity in Andean archaeology, Stovel notes, is the "vertical archipelago" model developed by John Murra. Vertical archipelagos are colonies sent by Andean communities to acquire resources in distant ecological zones, often on a higher or lower altitudinal floor and embedded within the territory of another "ethnic" group. The investigation of vertical archipelago or "complementarity" had stimulated much archaeological research into migration, colonization, and ethnicity, especially in southern Peru in the regions of Moquegua and the Osmore Drainage (Aldenderfer 1993; Buikstra 1995; Goldstein 2015; Owen 2005; Stanish 1992; Williams 2002).

Stovel finds that, despite decades of theoretical investment in the concept of ethnicity, Andean archaeology was still treating an ethnic group like the social scientist's "culture"—a group of people having a series of traits and practices observed by an external analyst to objectively separate culturally distinct groups into *cultures*. The peoples being classified, however, did not necessarily recognize the significance or the importance of these etically selected traits in their lived experience of constructing difference. Alternatively, Stovel (2012:10–14) cites laudable examples that represent "best practices" in Andean archaeology and favor a more theoretically informed and modern definition of ethnicity (see Reycraft 2005). Published after Stovel's article, George Lau's *Ancient Alterity in the Andes* (2013) also aims to gauge native Andeans' perception of difference rather than imposing an interpretation based purely on the archaeologist's classificatory scheme.

No amount of theoretical literature on ethnicity and Andean archaeology had prepared me for the surprises buried beneath Las Varas. Near the two entrances of the site, one facing the coast (west) and the other toward the highlands (east), we uncovered ritual structures that once received visitors coming from these opposite directions in the landscape. Associated features and artifacts provided more proof of the significance of these constructions: the ritual platform near the coastal entrance had the highest quantity of coastal-style pottery, whereas the plazas leading into the highlands were lined with highland-style cist tombs. This is like someone's house being decorated with souvenirs from New England in its east room and adorned with stuff from California in its west room. It is hard not to see the symbolic significance of these ritual structures' placement along the site's key boundary points. Such excavated results from Las Varas, to my knowledge, constitute unique archaeological evidence on how Andean people constructed ethnic boundaries utilizing ritual activity and architecture. A close example of this indexical signaling of ethnic or political affiliation through landscape orientation was found in the Arundane Temple, a Tiwanaku religious structure built within the Wari hilltop outpost of Cerro Baúl. Here, archaeologists recovered Tiwanaku incense burners near a platform that was oriented to the east—visually aligned to the mountains of Arundane in the direction of the Tiwanaku heartland (Williams and Nash 2006; 2016). Such findings, dramatic and exciting as they are, still need to be analyzed within a historically informed theoretical context.

Andean archaeologists were not, of course, the first in their discipline to study ethnicity. Archaeologists had been looking for ethnic groups since the very beginning of their discipline some two centuries ago, but their search ended disastrously: these early efforts projected nineteenth-century nationalistic ideals onto prehistoric tribes, the result being the construction of a fictitious past filled with culturally, linguistically, and racially pure peoples that European nascent states in their own time so desperately wanted to have. This was the tainted history of archaeology's venture into ethnicity. It was an ignominious legacy that scared off whole generations of archaeologists, convincing them that ethnicity could never and should never be approached with scientific objectivity. This book is an endeavor to disprove that belief.

The heavy historical baggage of "ethnicity studies" in archaeology is presented in chapter 1. My narrative is constructed as a point-counterpoint between two master tropes in anthropology, the staircase and the tree. It starts with the emergence of a nationalistic archaeology confident in its ability to track and find the ancient roots of modern nations. This aspiration was then deflated by a change in theoretical outlook following the conflagration of two world wars. Later, after the fall of European empires, even the belief in the homogeneity and stability of society became suspect. Ethnographers working in soon-to-be decolonized territories like Burma and Algeria recorded societies in flux where identities and ethnicities were constantly in the making. Such were the conditions that produced modern theories of ethnicity, and in this book I have chosen those of Barth, Bourdieu, and Rappaport to explain the construction of ethnic boundaries by ancient Andean communities. Regardless of one's theoretical choosing, I would hope that every reader understands the historical and empirical foundations that put into question any easy equations of archaeological culture with the ethnic group.

Chapter 2 returns to the Andes and offers an introduction to the *chaupiyunga*, a transitional zone consisting of warm valleys that connect the coast to the highlands. It has received scant archaeological investigations, even though in prehispanic and early colonial times it had been an area of intense ethnic interaction between coastal, highland, and chaupiyunga communities. Conflicts between ethnic groups were mythologized as the clash of the *huacas* (supernatural beings). One extraordinary document, the Huarochirí Manuscript, recorded these stories in Quechua, furnishing examples of highlanders displacing and sometimes incorporating "yunga" communities, all the while memorializing them by incorporating yunga culture and deities into highland rituals. The manuscript is the only book-length text written in Quechua that dates to the early colonial era, giving us a unique opportunity to hear tales of ethnic interaction in a native Andean voice.

Chapter 3 provides the ecological and environmental backdrop of the chaupiyunga zone in which Las Varas is found: the Middle Jequetepeque Valley of northern Peru. Surveys in the middle valley revealed a complicated network of prehispanic footpaths following quebradas (dry ravines) that branch off from the main river. These quebradas connect one valley to another and allow access into the highlands from the chaupiyunga. Las Varas is located at a juncture between the Jequetepeque River and a major quebrada heading into the highlands of Trinidad. Before describing our excavations, I outline the research design I had proposed for testing Murra's model of vertical archipelago at Las Varas. I utilized Stanish's methodology and archaeological expectations to determine whether colonization or trade better characterized the mode of resource acquisition in the Middle Jequetepeque Valley.

Chapters 4 and 5 are the archaeological meat of this book, as they deliver data from our excavations of the residential and ritual sectors. We opened the most excavation units in the residential sector (Sector 1), since the main objective of the project was to identify ethnic affiliation through domestic artifacts and architecture. Excavations of residential structures, described in chapter 4, uncovered houses built atop terraces. Some houses had a stone jamb next to their entrance, an architectural element reminiscent of the highlands. We recovered thousands of fragments of painted bowls classified in the literature as "Coastal Cajamarca" in addition to a type of domestic pottery similar to that of the Cajamarca highlands. Evidence from the residential sector indicated a chaupiyunga origin of the Coastal Cajamarca style, contrary to the hypothesis that it had come from the coast. Excavations of the domestic context proved to be incredibly productive and successful, but questions of ethnicity and boundary remained unanswered. It might appear that the residents of Las Varas had a "chaupiyunga" ethnic affiliation, but such a statement lacked information on how the village maintained its ethnic boundary and identity with surrounding communities.

Ritual structures near the entrances of Las Varas gave us the much-needed data on boundary construction. The Reception Platform was built next to the coastal entrance and contained the highest quantity of coastal-style pottery. It was remodeled several times, and chapter 5 details the sequence of its construction phases. The platform stood in clear contrast to the residential structures in having features like a central dedication stone and a bench buried in clean gravel. Given its unusual layout and fine quality of construction, it was most likely used for ritual. To the south of the site was a series of plazas laid out next to an opening into the Quebrada del Caracol, a natural corridor to the highlands of Trinidad. Highland-style cist tombs were placed next to the plazas, so that a traveler arriving from the highlands would be greeted by an open, ceremonial space consecrated by the remains of Las Varas's revered ancestors. Excavations in the platform and plazas demonstrated a strong association between ritual and community boundary. Examples from Andean archaeology, ethnohistory, and ethnography reveal a similar reliance on ritual to demarcate local and regional boundaries. In the case of Las Varas, these ritual boundaries meaningfully conveyed the ethnic affiliation of those entering the village, be they from the coast, chaupiyunga, or highlands. Although these ritual structures guarded the entrances of the site and monitored the flow of traffic, they were designed to be permeable so that residents and visitors could pass through and enter the community.

For instructors teaching a course on archaeological research strategies, chapters 4 and 5 could be assigned to two separate groups of students, that is, one group reads only chapter 4 and the other group only chapter 5. The two groups would then share their findings to see how excavating different contexts determines the outcome of an archaeological investigation.

The concluding chapter synthesizes the results from Las Varas with important implications for elucidating the culture history of the Jequetepeque Valley. By locating the origin of the Coastal Cajamarca style in the Middle Jequetepeque Valley, archaeologists are now able to recognize the chaupiyunga as an important agent in coast-highland interaction and detect its key role in guiding the valley's social and political development. In light of these findings, Murra's model could be refined to include the possibility that intermediate zones have mediated or even controlled interaction and exchange between the coast, highlands, and jungle. Data from Las Varas indicate that chaupiyunga settlers practiced both colonization and exchange to obtain coastal resources. Their ritual differentiated members of different ethnic groups, but it might also have stabilized ethnic relations through protocoled interactions. Histories of encounters between ethnic groups in the Andes and elsewhere in the world are often full of conflict and strife, but there are also instances of cooperation and peaceful exchange. Lacking fortifications and defensive works, Las Varas appears to have been on good, or at least acceptable, terms with neighboring communities and polities, and it is perhaps due to the potency of ritual as a medium of communication that information imbued with truth, sincerity, and sanctity could be transferred from one ethnic group to another.

1

The Staircase and the Tree

In the history of archaeology, the subject of ethnicity has twice piqued the discipline's interest: first as a project to trace the origin and migration of ancient peoples and later as part of the postprocessual attempt to locate prehistoric meaning and identity. The rise and fall of archaeology's interest in ethnicity resulted from a deep structural divide between two opposing, master metaphors in anthropology: the vertical ascent of social evolution, what Thomas Trautmann (1997:8) called the staircase trope, and the process of horizontal differentiation, or the divergence of cultures and languages as symbolized by the tree. The wavering between these two metaphors became a paradigmatic pendulum swinging between science and humanism, progressivism and relativity, objectivity and subjectivity, globalism and nationalism.

The staircase came out of the "rationalist thread, from Montesquieu through Morgan and Marx," while the tree, which stood for the uniqueness of each culture, was the "nationalist thread from Luther through Herder to Kossinna" (Sherratt 1989:162). Enlightenment thinkers embarked on projects to compare and rank human societies on a universal scale, but German philosopher Johann Gottfried Herder (1744–1803) argued for an *incommensurability* of cultures in that each culture could be understood only by its own logic rather than by cross-cultural comparisons. Yet Herder's nationalistic sympathies never polarized into ultranationalism; he defended the rights and uniqueness of every culture and rejected the ethnocentric belief that one nation was superior to another (Berlin 1976:186–189).

Gustaf Kossinna (1858–1931), nationalist archaeologist par excellence, did not share Herder's relativist ideals. Kossinna started his career as a philologist, completing his doctoral thesis on sound changes in Old High German (Kossinna 1881). He then shifted his research to the origins and development of the prehistoric Germans, a topic he believed was best approached by archaeology (Kossinna 1911:1–2).

For Kossinna, the geographic distribution of an archaeological culture was equivalent to the territory of a people, tribe, or, in its modern meaning, the ethnic group: "Sharply defined archaeological cultures [cultural provinces] always coincide with specific peoples or tribes" [*scharf umgrenzte archäologische Kulturprovinzen decken sich zu allen Zeiten mit ganz bestimmten Völkern oder Völkerstämmen*] (Kossinna 1911:3). Underlying this statement was the belief that prehistoric tribes acted like nation-states, and the assumptions made by this school of thought, known as culture-historical archaeology (Trigger 1989:148–186), are as follows:

1. An ethnic group is culturally homogeneous—that is, people in the group speak the same language, practice the same religion, and share the same beliefs and norms. There might be internal differences within the group, but differences within the group should be less than those between groups.

2. The materials and objects used by such an ethnic group or people are representative of their culture, so two archaeological sites with different materials would indicate the presence of two different cultures or ethnic groups.

3. An assemblage or collection of artifacts, called "archaeological culture," is therefore the physical trace or remains of a people. The archaeological culture directly reflects the once-living culture; hence the archaeological culture is equated with an ethnic group.

Kossinna did not pause to question why ethnic groups, past or present, should be so homogeneous. The geopolitical realities of Kossinna's nineteenth-century Europe deviated far from the ideal of a world populated by homogenous nation-states. In the half century before Kossinna's doctorate, seven new European nations had been created: Greece (1830), Belgium (1830–1839), Romania (1856), Italy (1859–1871), Germany (1864–1871), Bulgaria (1878), and Serbia (1867–1878). Kossinna's alma mater, the Friedrich-Wilhelms-Universität in Strassburg (now Strasbourg), was located in Alsace, a city and region whose nationhood shifted multiple times between France and Germany.

But Kossinna went further: he believed that archaeological cultures correlated with race and that certain cultures, the product of racial pedigree, were superior to others (Kossinna 1926). After his death in 1931, Kossinna's search for the roots of the Germanic people was taken up by the ancestral or heritage research unit, the Ahnenerbe, during World War II (Veit 1994:38). These views might seem extreme to us now, but Kossinna was not the only archaeologist of his era to have held these racial ideologies, nor was he the first to use archaeological materials to trace the origin, migration, and settlement of specific peoples (Trigger 1989:162–163).

European nationalism of the nineteenth and twentieth centuries produced romantic images of supposedly original peoples. Each country proclaimed the superiority and genius of its own *Volk*, as when Kossinna (1911) proclaimed the invention of bronze metallurgy, horse domestication, and writing by prehistoric Germans. World prehistory thus became the migration history of "great peoples" akin to that of "great men" (Carneiro 2000), providing narratives "aimed at distilling from archaeological remains a preliterate substitute for the conventional politico-military history, with cultures instead of statesmen as actors, and migrations in place of battles" (Childe 1958:70).

Then the pendulum swung from the tree to the staircase, from particular histories of specific tribes to the formulation of universal, human social evolution. In Britain, this momentus paradigm shift was instigated by archaeologist Vere Gordon Childe. The early Childe followed Kossinna's approach in tracing the prehistoric origins of historically documented people such as the Kelts, Teutons, Illyrians, and Slavs (Childe 1930). He often cited Kossinna as an authority on Central European cultures (e.g., Childe 1927:85, 88, 89, 142, 166, 168–180; Childe 1930:85, 242, 243) and wrote a favorable review of Kossinna's book, *Ursprung und Verbreitung der Germanen in vor- und frühgeschichtlicher Zeit* [Origin and Spread of the Germans in Pre- and Early History] (Childe 1927).

The threat of another world war galvanized Childe into writing "Is Prehistory Practical?" (1933), in which he argued against correlating race with archaeological culture and condemned the use of prehistory to fuel nationalistic sentiments. From then on, Childe abandoned what he called "bourgeois prehistory" that explained "each important technological advance or change in burial rite . . . by the assertion that it was 'introduced' by fresh 'invaders' from some generally remote and unknown cradle" (Childe 1942:342). The new Childe turned to social evolution, mixing Durkheimian functionalism with a Marxist emphasis on the modes of production (Childe 1936; 1950). Peter Gathercole (2009) suggested that this change of philosophy from bourgeois prehistory to social evolution was due in part to Childe's involvement with the Labour Party and the Left, experiences that would have acquainted him with the writings of Marx and other evolutionists.

Childe's evolutionary studies focused on two major transformations in prehistory: the adoption of agriculture and the emergence of cities, processes that he called the Neolithic and Urban Revolutions. For Childe, "what scientifically and practically serviceable anthropology ought to aim at is by observation and induction to establish rules showing how several variables change together and affect one another in changing—to be able to present, for instance, the kinship organization as a function of the technology or religion as a function of the family and so on" (Childe 1946:248). In setting aside the *particular* ethnic histories of specific tribes for an understanding of a *universal* history—the evolution of human societies—Childe swung archaeology back toward the trope of the staircase.

Cultural evolutionism, initiated by nineteenth-century scholars like Herbert Spencer, Lewis Henry Morgan, and E. B. Tylor, was revived in the 1950s by American anthropologist Leslie White, another scholar whose involvement with the Left and the Socialist Labor Party was at the time politically incorrect (Peace 2007:82–91). As interests in social evolution faded in cultural anthropology, the torch was passed to archaeologists keen to use an evolutionary framework to understand the many millennia of sociocultural change. Archaeologist Lewis Binford spearheaded the New Archaeology movement that heralded explicit hypotheses and scientific laws to understand cultural systems and their evolution (Binford 1962). Childe and Binford are currently the leading contenders in academic journals and the blogosphere for the title "Most Influential Archaeologist of the Twentieth Century" (Smith 2009; Kelly 2011).

Impermeable Billiard Balls

After World War II, the decline of the British Empire would likewise dethrone its dominant anthropological paradigm, structural-functionalism. This school of thought posited a stable relationship between different components or segments of a society, with the purpose or "function" of society being the maintenance of its own stability and equilibrium. Functionalists believed that certain cultural practices like taboos or rituals served to create cohesion and integration within the group. Even Marvin Harris, no fan of postmodern reflexivity, noticed the resemblance between the functionalist's stable society and an empire's orderly colony: "It is impossible not to draw a connection between the proposal to study social systems *as if* they were solidary and *as if* they were timeless, with sponsorship, employment, and indirect association of the members of [the structural-functional] school by and with a now defunct colonial system" (Harris 1968:516; emphasis in original).

The death of structural-functionalism made way for important anthropological works on social change, agency, and ethnicity. Raymond Firth advocated a "dynamic approach" to the analysis of social change, and Firth's student, Edmund Leach, wrote the influential *Political Systems of Highland Burma* (1954) that overturned the functionalist paradigm, effectively dismembering the once coherent entity of culture/society/ethnicity.

In 1939, a 29-year-old Leach went to the highlands of northern Burma to carry out his doctoral research on the social and political organization of the Kachin. At that time, two types of political organization characterized Kachin settlements: autonomous, independent villages on the one hand, and clusters of villages ruled by a single chief on the other. A third kind of political organization—stratified, hierarchical kingdoms—characterized the Shan, a neighboring group. The main language of the Shan was Tai, whereas the Kachin spoke non-Tai languages including Jinghpaw, Maru, Nung, and Lisu. At the time of Leach's ethnography, many Kachins practiced spirit and ancestor worship. By contrast, "all Shans are Buddhists" (Leach 1954:30). Shan kingdoms were located in the lowland valleys, and their agricultural production was based on irrigated rice paddies. Kachin villagers, who occupied mostly the rugged hills, practiced both terrace irrigation and slash-and-burn (*taungya*) cultivation.

To an outsider visiting the highlands of northern Burma, the Kachin and Shan would appear to be two distinct cultural or ethnic groups, differing in language, religion, mode of agriculture, and political system. Some colonial documents even classified Kachin and Shan as separate "races" (Leach 1954:20, 43). But the ethnic categories of "Shan" and "Kachin" did not form hard, impenetrable boundaries: Kachin individuals sometimes became Shan, and some Shan became Kachin. Hpaka Lung Hseng was a 79-year-old man classified by the colonial Court of Enquiry as "racially" Lahtawng Kachin. His life story, however, revealed a more complicated scenario: "When I was a boy some 70 years ago, the (Shan) Regent Sao Hkam Hseng who then reigned in Mong Mao sent a relative of his, Nga Hkam by name, to negotiate an alliance with the Kachins of Mong Hko. After a while Nga Hkam settled down in Pao Mo and later he exchanged names with my ancestor Hko Tso Li and my grandfather Ma Naw, then Duwas of Pao Mo; *after that we became Shans and Buddhists* and prospered greatly and, as members of the Hkam clan, whenever we went to Mong Mao we stayed with the Regent, conversely in Mong Hko our house was theirs" (Leach 1954:2; emphasis mine).

Realizing the complexity and subtlety of ethnic labels in highland Burma, Leach commented, "It appears that this witness considered that for the past 70 years or so all his family have been simultaneously Kachins and Shans. As a Kachin the witness was a member of the Pawyam lineage of the Lahtaw(ng) clan. As a Shan he was a Buddhist, and a member of the Hkam clan, the royal house of the Möng Mao State." Appendix I of Leach's book provided five more examples of individuals and groups changing their linguistic and cultural affiliation.

Shan and Kachin populations did not form two discrete, separate territories. Instead, Shan and Kachin settlements interspersed with each other, with Shan kingdoms in the valleys and Kachin villages in the mountains, so that a Shan kingdom would neighbor a Kachin community that was bordered, on the other side, by another Shan kingdom, and so on. This intermixing of Shan and

Kachin communities between valleys and mountains created a crazy quilt of variegated ethnicities, cultures, and languages across the northern Burmese landscape (Leach 1954:Map 3).

Adding to the complexity of Shan-Kachin relations was the unstable nature of Kachin politics. As mentioned, Kachin villages oscillated between chiefly clusters (*gumsa*) and independent settlements (*gumlao*). Gumsa was a hierarchical system in which a hereditary chief ruled several villages, whereas gumlao, a more egalitarian arrangement, was characterized by independent villages that could not demand labor or tribute from each other. Gumsa chiefs acted like aristocrats and collected tribute in the form of prime cuts of meat like the thighs of a buffalo or pig. The chief can also demand labor from the villagers and press them into preparing the chief's field or building his house. Aspiring leaders in the gumlao or egalitarian system used political guile and strategy to make themselves into gumsa chiefs. Discontent villagers under the yoke of gumsa would then rebel and revert back to the leveled playing field of gumlao. Kachin society therefore fluctuated between gumsa and gumlao, a situation analogous to a society that switches back and forth between democracy and authoritarian rule or, in Leach's terms, republicanism and monarchy (Leach 1954:197).

Because of these findings, Leach no longer believed in the "society in equilibria" model envisioned by the structural-functionalists. The ethnic categories of "Shan" and "Kachin" did not form hard, impenetrable boundaries: individuals could change their identities. The ethnic landscape was multilingual and multicultural. There was no simple co-occurrence of language, culture, and political system. These attributes did not come neatly packaged as a single "ethnic group."

Speaking directly to the archaeologists, Leach railed against the migrationist paradigm in his essay "Aryan Invasion over Four Millennia" (1990). He questioned all attempts to link language with archaeological culture and reached the devastating conclusion that "the Aryan invasion never happened at all" (Leach 1990:245). Putting forth objections already raised in *Highland Burma*, Leach criticized how archaeologists "seem to assume that cultural systems and language systems are bonded together and intrinsically stable over long periods of time." This type of thinking treated culture as "impermeable billiard balls" that, like barbarian hordes, would simply sweep across the prehistoric landscape while remaining intact and unchanged (Leach 1990:241).

Other anthropologists have similarly questioned the existence of the homogenous tribe. Morton Fried, an American anthropologist interested in social evolution, wrote *The Notion of Tribe* (1975) to reject the bounded, closed-system view of the quintessential "tribe." According to Fried, the notion that human groups once formed "tribes"—bounded, monolingual, monocultural, endogamous (in-marrying)—was a myth created by colonial administrators and modern anthropologists. Fried presented ethnographic data, chapter by chapter, detailing "tribal" political, cultural, linguistic, and marriage practices, to refute the stereotype that non-state societies (e.g., those of native North America or Melanesia) were homogenous. He provided multiple examples to show that the anthropologist's tribe was in reality multilingual communities that traded and intermarried extensively with neighboring tribes, leading to open networks of ritual and political exchange.

The idea of the bounded tribe is still popular today. In contemporary usage, the words "tribal" and "tribalism" carry a connotation of unruly divisiveness and primitiveness, characteristics that pundits like to condemn as a danger to civil discourse and global integration. This stereotype of the tribe—an isolated, ethnocentric group of people waging a Hobbesian war of all against all—was a primitivist myth that postwar anthropologists were trying to debunk.

The conflagration of the last world war concluded, for the most part, racist theories in anthropology. With European empires contracting and former colonies nationalizing, the once safe and stable billiard balls shattered. After Boas, the concept of culture lost its association with race; after Leach, it lost its connotation as a coherent and stable group; after Fried, it lost its status as a homogenous tribe; and after Fredrik Barth (to be discussed in the next section), it would no longer be equated with "ethnicity." It was as if social scientists had disassembled, as one would a car or computer, the imagined theoretical ideal of a society, only to put it back together, piece by piece, to understand it better.

A Game of Poker

> "And then I met Edmund Leach and I think
> it took two hours and I fell in love."
> —Interview with Fredrik Barth, June 5, 2005 (Barth and Anderson 2007:iv)

Such was the impact of Fredrik Barth's *Ethnic Groups and Boundaries* (1969) that periods before and after its publication were christened "B.B." and "A.B"—Before and After Barth (Despres 1975:189). In 1967 (Year 2 B.B.), a symposium was held at the University of Bergen to discuss the issues of ethnic groups, interaction, and boundaries. Barth, organizer of the conference, later edited papers from the symposium and published them in *Ethnic Groups and Boundaries: The Social Organization of Culture Difference*. Barth (2007:10) acknowledged Leach's *Highland Burma* as an inspiration for the conference: "Inspired by Leach's monograph on the Kachin, I assumed that some of my Scandinavian colleagues had data with which we could modify conventional anthropological assumptions about the congruence of our categories of tribe = culture = society. So our symposium topic became ethnicity. I circulated a brief discussion of issues and concepts with my invitation to the symposium, and we ended up with seven ethnographic cases, in addition to my introduction, in our resulting publication." Leach had been Barth's PhD advisor at the University of Cambridge (Eriksen 2015:38), and two aspects of Barth's thinking reflected Leach's influence: (1) ethnic identity and boundary are not "natural" or naturally occurring categories, and therefore they require explanation, and (2) actors make strategic decisions to sustain or alter ethnic and other social categories.

The collection of essays in *Ethnic Groups* "addresses itself to the problems of ethnic groups and their persistence" (Barth 1969a:9). The puzzle or problem of persistence is not that ethnic groups are isolated and cut off from each other but precisely the opposite—they are in constant contact with each other, but at the same time they maintain or "persist in" their boundaries:

> First, it is clear that boundaries persist despite a flow of personnel across them. In other words, categorical ethnic distinctions do not depend on an absence of mobility, contact and information, but do entail social processes of exclusion and incorporation whereby discrete categories are maintained despite changing participation and membership in the course of individual life histories. Secondly, one finds that stable, persisting, and often vitally important social relations are maintained across such boundaries, and are frequently based precisely on the dichotomized ethnic statuses. In other words, ethnic distinctions do not depend on an absence of social interaction and acceptance, but are quite to the contrary often the very foundations on which embracing social systems are built. Interaction in such a social system does not lead to its liquidation through change and acculturation; cultural differences can persist despite inter-ethnic contact and interdependence. (Barth 1969a:9–10)

Each essay in Barth's *Ethnic Groups* was an attempt at solving the problem of boundary persistence. Barth's case study concerned the Swat Valley Pathans of Pakistan, a Pashto-speaking group neighbored by the Baluch, Hazara, Panjab, and Kohistani (Barth 1969b). Criteria such as language, religion, and set of ethics underlay Pathan ethnicity. Like the Kachin of highland Burma, there were incidences of personnel leakage or identity shift when Pathans became Baluch, Panjabi, or Hazara. For instance, Pathan individuals pressed into Baluch chiefdom as a result of war or crime would discard their Pathan identity. Since a necessary condition for being Pathan was political independence and egalitarianism, anybody submitting to Baluch rule would, by default, give up their Pathan-ness and effectively turn Baluch. "It is to the advantage of the actors themselves to change their label so as to avoid the costs of failure" (Barth 1969b:133), the costs being the social shame of a Pathan's liberty lost.

A fine illustration of tribal boundaries maintained through interaction was furnished by Ian Hodder's ethnographic study of material culture in the Baringo District of Western Kenya (Hodder 1977; 1982). Here he recorded the distribution of various materials and their styles among three tribes, the Njemps (or Ilchamus), Tugen, and Pokot. When Hodder plotted the presence/absence of Baringo artifacts on a map, items like ear ornaments, four-legged stools, baskets, bowls, and honeypots indeed followed tribal lines and were used only by a certain tribe. Things that crossed boundaries, however, were (1) people (marriage partners), (2) language, and (3) objects like spears and decorated calabashes. Intertribal marriage was frequent, and people living near tribal boundaries often spoke two languages or more. Moreover, a general style of spears and incised calabash designs was shared by all three tribes. Spears and calabashes were potent symbols of tension between young men and their elders, between women and older men, and therefore these styles permeated tribal boundaries. Hodder's Baringo study exemplified Barthian principles.

Barth's interest in an actor's strategy could again be traced to Leach. In *Highland Burma*, Leach noted the strategic or gamelike behavior of Kachin individuals during ceremonial exchanges: "In some ways *hpaga* [exchangeable wealth objects] can be thought of as analogous to the individual cards used in a game of poker. One ritual context calls for the production of four aces, another for a royal flush—the cards are valuable only in their context" (Leach 1954:154). For Leach, "the proper analogy for human behaviour is not natural law—of a physical kind—but a game of chess. The field of play and the rules of the game are laid out in advance but the way the game is played out is unpredictable" (Leach 1973:764).

Whereas Leach merely invoked game as a metaphor, Barth applied game theory, the mathematical approach to interactive strategic decisions and actions, to understand the political process of Pathan bloc formation. In his article "Segmentary Opposition and the Theory of Games" (1959), Barth took von Neumann and Morgenstern's (1944:222–225) equation of the "zero-sum simple majority game" to calculate the theoretical values, or costs and benefits, of switching bloc alliances. This article was the first in anthropology to utilize game theory, and even now, some 60 years later, I could find only one other article (Davenport 1960) and one archaeology monograph (Stanish 2017:166–184) that use game theory to analyze anthropological data.

To summarize Barth's argument: within a village, there are two opposing "blocs" or *dela*. Each bloc is trying to overwhelm the other by having a majority of members to win decisions and resources at meetings, councils, and other spheres of contest. Furthermore, each bloc has a chief that receives an added "bonus" that is not so much material gain as prestige. The goal of the "losing" or minority bloc, then, is to entice and bribe members of the majority with offers of chieftainship, goading them to defect and join the minority bloc. Once the minority bloc gains more members than the other bloc, the tables turn. A real historical winner of this game was Miangul Gulshahzada Abdul Wadud, who, between 1917 and 1927, adopted a strategy of joining the weaker bloc to gain control over a large part of the Swat Valley and ultimately became the founder of the Swat State (Barth 1959:19).

In "Segmentary Opposition," Barth explains the presence of dual blocs within each village by modeling actors' self-interests and their political consequences. His approach has a very important implication for anthropology: certain social structures, rather than being the result of some innate symbolic or cultural code, are in fact the emergent properties of interactive and strategic actions. This is a crucial insight, for game theory allows analysts to envision nondeterministic outcomes resulting from human interactions. A mathematical or quantitative approach is often stereotyped, erroneously, as mechanistic and deterministic, but game theory actually takes into account tremendous variations and inexhaustible iterations of actors' strategic decisions. For example, the number of ways to play chess or poker is astronomical, but if we do not understand the rules and the tactics, we will never be able to explain the recurrence of certain moves and countermoves lest we mystify them as "cultural structure."

Like Leach's *Highland Burma*, which sees dynamic instability as the key to recurrent social forms, Barth's game theory analysis lies at that rare intersection between strategy, structure, individual interests, and unintended organization. At Leach's encouragement, Barth submitted his essay to the Royal Anthropological Institute's Curl Prize competition; it did not win because the committee deemed Barth's work "not sufficiently respectful of Evans-Pritchard" (Barth 2007:4). Game theory offends anthropological ancestors still.

Playing the Field

Leaving Anglo-American traditions, I want to connect Leach's and Barth's interests in strategy and game theory with the works of Pierre Bourdieu. Having cut his ethnographic teeth in turbulent mid-century French Algeria, Bourdieu became fascinated by the importance of strategy and game in creating social relations and structure: "Science must know that it does nothing more than record, in the form of tendential laws, the logic which characterizes *a certain game, at a certain moment in time*, and which functions in favor of those who dominate the game and have the means to set the rules of the game in fact and in law" (Bourdieu and Wacquant 1992:197, footnote 158, emphasis in the original).

Bourdieu developed concepts like *habitus* and *field* to resolve what he perceived as the impasse between Lévi-Straussian structural determinism and the free-will philosophy of Sartre. On the one hand is Sartre's vision of unconstrained individualism, which "can break out of the absolute discontinuity of choices without past or future only by the free resolution of a pledge and self-loyalty or by the free abdication of bad faith" (Bourdieu 1990:43). On the other is French structuralism, whose reliance on binary cultural logic influenced Bourdieu's essay on the Kabyle house (1970) written for a Festschrift dedicated to Lévi-Strauss. "The Kabyle House" enjoyed widespread citation and no lack of reprints, even though Bourdieu later critiqued it as being confined within "the limits of structuralist thought" (Bourdieu 1990:316–317, note 1).

To subvert the opposition between objectivism and subjectivism, Bourdieu began developing concepts like field, habitus, and practice to escape this tiring dichotomy. For him, society is not an impermeable billiard ball but a connection of relations channeled by what he called the *habitus*, defined as the "systems of durable, transposable dispositions, structured structures predisposed to function as structuring structures, that is, as principles of the generation and structuring of practices and representations" (Bourdieu 1977:72; 1990:52). This definition has perhaps left many readers (this one included) wondering—what exactly are "structured structures" or "structuring structures"?

If I understand him correctly, habitus are repetitive behaviors whose very repetition deepens the chances of that behavior being repeated. This was termed "deuterolearning" by Gregory Bateson and Roy Rappaport: "More important to our discussion are propositions that come out of what Bateson in his earlier work (1951) called 'deuterolearning,' a form of learning very much like, if not identical with, what Harlow called 'set-learning' (1949), and rather similar to what much later (1977) Bourdieu called 'habitus.' Deutero-learning is 'second-order' learning: generalizing extrapolation from 'first-order' learning, which is the learning of particular facts or tasks. In learning a set of nonsense syllables, for instance, a subject not only learns that set of nonsense syllables but also learns how to learn sets of nonsense syllables" (Rappaport 1999:304). Such structuring of behavior is like the geological process of a valley forming, where continuous water stream cuts and deepens a channel that would, in turn, direct future flows.

Is habitus always unconscious behavior? Not necessarily, since Bourdieu also associates habitus with taste and distinction: "The habitus is both the generative principle of objectively classifiable judgments and the system of classification (*principium divisionis*) of these practices. It is in the relationship between the two capacities which define the habitus, the capacity to produce classifiable practices and works, and the capacity to differentiate and appreciate practices and products (taste), that the represented social world, i.e., the space of life-styles, is constituted" (Bourdieu 1984:170). Certain practices are classified and judged, forming "taste." For Bourdieu, taste is the vital ingredient in creating social categories—classificatory schemes underlying the construction of gender, class, and ethnicity.

Anthropologists and archaeologists have been attracted to Bourdieu's practice theory in order to investigate ethnicity (Bentley 1987; Jones 1997:117). Practice theorists want to turn the structural-functionalist paradigm on its head: not that structure determines practice, but that practice creates social categories. As foreshadowed by Sartre's bleak (or optimistic?) assessment of the proletariat class, "The nineteenth-century worker makes himself what he is, that is, he practically and rationally determines the order of his expenditure . . . and by his freedom he makes himself what he is, what he was, what he must be" (Sartre 1960:294; cited in Bourdieu 1990:44). "Practice archaeologists" view activities as the key to generating social structure, while artifacts or artifact style, traditionally the "fossil index" of culture and society, now serves as a complement, or better, an indirect inference, to our data on prehistoric practices. The old approach saw artifacts or artifact style as products of a monolithic society, the impermeable billiard ball. The new approach, which I advocate, sees activities and practices as the sinews of social relations that lead to structures and categories.

Actors carry out the habitus not out of blind faith or obedience to a deterministic structure but within a *field* where, like the sports arena, strategy and tactics matter. Here again is that metaphor of poker, game, and cards: "The matrimonial game is similar to a card game, in which the outcome depends partly on the deal, the cards held (their value itself being defined by the rules of the game, characteristic of the social formation in question), and partly on the players' skill: that is to say, firstly on the material and symbolic capital possessed by the families concerned . . . and secondly on the competence which enables the strategists to make the best use of this capital" (Bourdieu 1977:58). This aspect of the habitus—negotiated outcomes of idiosyncratic decisions or contingent strategies operating in the field—has been passed over by social scientists in favor of a more deterministic, structural interpretation. But to understand habitus we should instead go back to Bourdieu's original intent in discussing structure alongside the strategic or gamelike aspects of the field.

Practice theory is not panacea: it does not explain why certain practices or activities should structure people's lives, nor does it explain why some practices are more powerful than others in shaping the social world. Practice theorists often treat habitus as a flat terrain in the topography of causation. In other words, they frequently invoke habitus as an explanation for any kind of behavior. Why did this person choose to dine in this restaurant? Habitus. Why did this person play this song? Habitus. Going back to the geology metaphor—if there is a dip or valley that channels the flow of human action in a certain direction, we need a historical or structural-generative framework to explain how that geological feature (e.g., river, canyon, glacial moraine) came to form in the first place. Indeed anthropologist Roy Rappaport argues that a particular kind of practice—ritual—can act as a potent factor, like a powerful current, that channels people's actions into creating social boundaries.

Analog to Digital: The Role of Ritual

As important as habitus or deutero-learning is to human sociocultural life, Rappaport (1999:307) expressed doubt that any society can successfully operate by habitus only: "It is simply this: in no society does everyone have the same life experiences. Each person, therefore, is likely to extrapolate somewhat unique sets of generalizations from his or her unique experiences. Each person's deutero-truths [assumptions about the world acquired from habitus or deuteron-learning] may be expected to differ in some degree from those of others, even of the same society or, for that matter, even of the same family. It would therefore be extremely difficult or impossible for any society to found convention and to insure orderly social life on the ground of deutero-learning alone and, in fact, no society does." If habitus is idiosyncratic, then it risks ephemerality; thus there should be a mode of social action that surpasses mere deutero-learning, and this special kind of action should be of greater strength, etch a deeper mark, and leave a longer-lasting impression in the formation and enforcement of social structures. For Rappaport (1999:24) this would be *the performance of more or less invariant sequences of formal acts and utterances not entirely encoded by the performers*: ritual.

Rappaport's theory of ritual has often been stereotyped as ecological functionalism, but that is an inaccurate characterization (see Rappaport 1999:28). His ideas are more akin to cybernetic or information theory, closer to Marshall McLuhan than to Marvin Harris. Rappaport (1999:455–456) would readily admit that certain beliefs could be maladaptive or destructive to society and environment. In his final work, *Ritual and Religion in the Making of Humanity* (1999), Rappaport explored how the structure and form of ritual, which he believed to be a unique medium of communication, determine the nature and quality of the information conveyed. The defining properties of ritual (invariant sequence, performance by participants) index social information and relay messages of greater truthfulness, enshrining unfalsifiable absolute truths by shielding them with "sanctity" (Rappaport 1999:281).

These formal properties of ritual, with their informational consequences, result in rather important social effects: (1) creation of discrete, *digital* social categories, (2) demarcation of space and time, and (3) self-referencing of individuals within those constructed socio-natural landscapes. These consequences, as I argue in this book, are potent factors in the creation of ethnic boundaries.

Digital categories. Social life is full of ambiguities and murkiness, and in response we chop up gradients of human differences into hard categories; it is we who divide continua of space-time into sharply defined territories and neat calendars. With the passing of just one second on Tuesday 11:59:59 pm, for example, we enter Wednesday. In Rappaport's theory of ritual, reality's gradients are *analog* signals, in the sense that there is no hard break between subtle shades of gray along a continuum. By contrast, *digital* signals have no such ambiguity. They are binary and therefore operate like a switch that turns on/off, black/white, in/out, 1/0. One of the functions of ritual is the digitization or recognition of social categories that turns shades of analog differences into hard, digital boundaries (Rappaport 1999:91). This means that clear-cut, black-or-white categories are established as opposed to ambiguous states that grade into each other. In an initiation rite, for instance, a child becomes an adult; he goes from one discrete category to another no matter what his actual biological state of maturation. Social or ethnic groups (as I argue in the next chapter) are digitally recognized during rituals, especially in cases where social groups march in a linear procession, in a sequence that presents the groups one by one. During this kind of procession, the groups substantiate the reality of their groupings by performing their "groupness" and signaling their identities to participants and witnesses. The modern analogy of this would be the Olympics opening ceremony where all the athletes march, one country after another, into the stadium.

Demarcation of space and time. Rituals often refer to points in the landscape and mark divisions in time. The Tewa winter chief monitors where the sun sets on the northern New Mexico horizon during winter solstice (Ortiz 1969:102); a llama herder in Ayacucho sprinkles chicha (corn beer) in the direction of the wamani, the animate mountain (Flannery et al. 1989:154). Such references to places in the landscape are important because they frequently allude to the homeland or origin place of ethnic groups, to their boundaries, or to their patron deity. And if myths are invoked, these narratives refer to a distant past when ancestors founded a lineage or ethnic group. Since the timing of rituals almost always syncs with the agricultural cycle, ethnic groups occupying different environmental zones, with different crops and staples, will follow different ritual calendars and celebrate different ceremonies. Thus the "digitizing" effects of ritual not only establish social categories but also link those categories to points in space (landmarks, shrines, cardinal directions) and time (annual ceremonies, sacred calendars).

Self-reference. Having established one's place in the physical and social world, ritual allows participants to "self-reference," that is, "express the individual's status as a social person in the structural system in which he finds himself for the time being" (Leach 1954:10–11). During ritual, a person's status is either explicitly or implicitly stated: children become adults during an initiation ceremony (age status); a herder thanks the mountains for taking care of his flock (the status of giver vs. recipient in the environment); athletes represent their nations during sports competitions (nationality). We academics cannot avoid the self-referencing effects of our particular ritual, the academic conference. In highly structured sessions of papers and presentations, speakers go on stage to recite information imbued with truth and sanctity, the same information that, if overheard in a bar or in the kitchen, would not have carried the same weight. The participants in these conferences constantly transmit self-referential messages through nametags and conversations, clarifying their institutional affiliation, educational status, paradigmatic allegiances, mentorship genealogy, and so on. Previous achievements are celebrated in ceremonies like the "Special Recognition Award," and new statuses are made by testing an individual's intellectual and professional prowess through a particularly traumatic rite known as the job interview.

Ritual not only hardens social boundaries but also provides a diplomatic protocol for mediating intergroup interaction. Were multiple groups to forge alliances and establish peace, the repetitive, structured nature of ritual helps to cement trust and sanctify transactions. I further elaborate this argument in chapters 5 and 6.

I do not want to imply that every ritual practice or action is stable and enduring. Ritual interactions are fraught with risks of failure (Hüsken 2007; Keane 1997:27). The 1906 episode of Orayvi village fission happened just two days after the Snake Dance, a major Hopi ceremony (Whiteley 2008:10). Returning to the parlance of information theory, if a ritual was completely rigid and unchanging, so that "each ritual . . . allows no uncertainty, no choice," then that ritual, "in the statistical sense of information theory" conveys "no information from sender to receiver" (Wallace 1966:233). Any ritual that does not perturb in response to the ever-changing natural, social, political, or artistic world would ultimately shrivel into a useless, boring activity.

Ethnicity Is Relational Interaction

The archaeologist at the beginning of the introduction, after returning from fieldwork, after reviewing the literature, now feels the burden of theory in trying to interpret the evidence on ethnicity in prehistory. How can archaeologists study ethnicity? The lessons from previous investigations are as follows:

1. Archaeologists once tried to find culturally, linguistically, and even racially homogeneous groups or tribes—equivalents of idealized nation-states—in prehistory (Kossinna).

2. Anthropologists, through detailed ethnographic fieldwork, revealed that such linguistically and culturally pure groups were rare before modern nation-states (Fried, Leach) and that such homogeneous groups were likely the imaginary products of colonial governments.

> 3. Still, even if these groups were heterogeneous and internally diverse, we nonetheless have examples of societies maintaining ethnic boundaries, but with people, materials, and ideas constantly flowing through those boundaries (Barth, Hodder). In other words, ethnicity is a result of interaction and not isolation. Ethnicity is not the natural state of human affairs but a cultural construct and a historical process.
>
> 4. We need to understand the practices that create social groups, structures, categories, and boundaries (Bourdieu). Oftentimes the decisions behind these practices are made strategically in order to secure scarce resources or social positions; a complex network of interactive strategic decisions can lead to unexpected structural configurations (Barth).
>
> 5. Certain practices, however, are more powerful than others in shaping identity. Ritual, because of its ability to signal discrete or digital categories (Rappaport), is an important factor in reinforcing ethnic boundaries.

For archaeologists, the main challenge is how to document ethnic self-ascription. If ethnicity is based on an individual's self-identification, then what hopes do we have in finding ethnicity besides reading that person's diary? Indeed, in the history of archaeological theory, the problem of subjective meaning pushed the paradigmatic pendulum back to the metaphor of the tree, back to particular cultures and histories under the rallying cry of "postprocessual" archaeology. Hodder's (1982) monograph on Baringo material culture was a major contribution to the archaeology of ethnicity since it examined horizontal differentiation—social or ethnic differences—from the perspective of objects and interactions. And it is no coincidence that processual archaeology, associated with the staircase metaphor, tended to focus on topics of vertical differentiation such as rank and stratification. I would venture that Hodder, who spearheaded the postprocessual movement, started considering issues of subjectivity and meaning when he was confronted, ethnographically, with the material implications of boundary and identity.

We need not choose sides in dichotomized positions of the objective/subjective and the internal/external. Bourdieu obsessed over this problem, and his solution came in the observation that subjective categories, perceived and internalized by individuals, have to be performed or externalized so that others, too, can recognize them (Bourdieu 1977:3–9; see similar reasoning on the "externalization" of ideology by DeMarrais et al. 1996). If these externalizations of subjective categories, especially ethnic ones, have material implications, we as archaeologists can be optimistic. Some archaeologists have proposed that artifacts found in household or private settings are more indicative of ethnic identity (Aldenderfer 1993; Stanish 1989); this proposition is tested and discussed in chapter 4. Alternatively, I argue that ritual spaces and activities are also useful avenues for archaeologists to find traces of ethnic boundaries (chapter 5).

Let us set aside, for now, the issue of how deeply archaeologists can delve into the prehistoric mind (though I profess my skepticism of claims of harmonic empathy with ancient peoples). The crucial first step is to correctly identify patterns in the archaeological record, specifically, which variables covary with others. For example, round houses always (or almost always) have stone doors, female burials always have necklaces, or pots on the west side of the river are always painted blue. When proven, these associations are, at the very least, meaningful to the analyst, the archaeologist. And one can argue *only later* that perhaps these patterns had been meaningful for those who made the artifacts. These repetitive patterns then acquire an important contrast against another archaeological culture whose square houses have no doors, where both male and female burials include necklaces, and where, on this side of the river, pots are painted green.

We need to conceptualize ethnic markers in archaeology not as objective traits or characteristics but as meaningful elements that provide contrast with the "other." A proper archaeological investigation of ethnicity should reveal the differences and interaction between two or more groups. In other words, an adequate documentation of ethnicity is not just a simple statement of "A does this and B does that"; it should include an exposition of what happens when "A meets B." This relational definition of ethnicity forces us to examine contact and interaction as the hallmarks of ethnicity.

One of the goals of this book is to demonstrate that it is possible for archaeologists to document ethnicity and ethnic processes using only the archaeological record. The archaeological evidence should be seen as a "standalone system" that can operate independently, that is, free from the crutches of historical sources or ethnographic analogies. Still, we do have Spanish and native eyewitness accounts of indigenous ethnic groups in the Andes; some of these documents, to be discussed in the following chapter, record ritual and ethnic encounters in the Andean *chaupiyunga*, an ecological zone between the coast and the highlands that was once the hotbed of ethnic interaction. These groups in the chaupiyunga confronted each other in myths and colonial-period courts, and while their actions meet the criterion of ethnicity as meaningful relations, they also reveal unique Andean ways of making and perceiving ethnic difference.

2

Ethnic Encounters in the Andean Chaupiyunga

On the western coast of South America is a thin strip of desert, one of the three major environmental zones of the Central Andes: coast (*costa*), highland (*sierra*), and jungle (*selva*). Sandwiched between the coast and the highlands is a transition zone, the *yunga* or *chaupiyunga*, where veins of river connect the mountain to the sea.

Sixteenth-century Spanish chronicler Pedro de Cieza de León provided some of the earliest written descriptions of the yunga:

> In many parts of the sierra where the rivers flow, as the sierras are very high, the plains are sheltered and temperate, so much so that in many places it is hot, as it is on these plains. The people who live there, even though they are in the sierra, are known as Yungas; and throughout Peru, when they allude to these warm, sheltered regions that lie among the sierras, they say, "It is Yunga," and the inhabitants have no other name, even though their settlements and regions have names. Thus those who live in the regions I have referred to, and those who dwell in these plains and coastal regions of Peru, are called Yungas because they live in hot country. (Cieza de León 1959 [1553]:306)
>
> Beyond these, in the lowlands, are the dwellings of Chan-Chan, which, as they lie in the hot country, are called by the natives Yungas, which means "hot country." As it never snows or is very cold here, trees and other things thrive which are not to be found in cold climates. For this reason all those living in hot or warm valleys or regions are called Yungas, as they are known today and will be, even though centuries elapse. (Cieza de León 1959 [1553]:66–67)

In Cieza's account, yunga is a climatic zone rather than a specific place; the term does not distinguish whether these warm lands are on the western or eastern slope of the Andes, or whether it is on the coast or in a highland valley. Why this lack of specificity?

Ethnic or environmental descriptors in the Andes are *relational* rather than specific. The yunga person is someone living in a lower elevation zone, in a place that is warm and filled with exotic fruits and animals, where people speak a different language, wear weird clothes, and perform strange ceremonies.

This chapter provides the environmental and cultural background to the *chaupiyunga* zone, invoked here specifically as the valleys and foothills on the *western* slope of the Andes, between the coastal plain and the highlands. This area has received less archaeological attention than the coast or the highlands, even though the chaupiyunga, where different ethnic groups once came into contact, is an ideal site for studying ethnicity in the Andes.

I first provide a brief environmental and archaeological background of the chaupiyunga before presenting two ethnohistorical cases from central Peru: (1) a manuscript written in Quechua from the province of Huarochirí that recounts mythical and ritual encounters between the highlands and the chaupiyunga and (2) a series of litigations from the Chillón Valley that reveals the complicated shuffling of ethnic groups by the Inca Empire. The first case concerns mythical matters, the second legal. Both give us insights into the interaction between ethnic groups in the Andean chaupiyunga, an area where archaeological information might be lacking, but early colonial documents offer us native visions of life, ritual, and ethnicity.

Chaupiyunga: Environment and Prehistory

The chaupiyunga is a warm and sunny zone that receives slightly more rain than the arid coast but still not enough precipitation for rainfall agriculture. Fields in the chaupiyunga are irrigated by canals, the bulk of their water arriving between December and March, a time of rain in the highlands. Mid-valley vegetation is similar to that of the coast, with subtropical plants such as cane stalks (*Gynerium sagittatum*), shrubs (*Capparis angulata*), and trees (*Prosopis pallida, Bursera graveolens, Inga feuillei, Sambucus peruviana*) growing in well-watered areas near the river, next to canals, and in small garden plots. The prized plant of the chaupiyunga is a variety of coca cultivated on the western slopes of the Andes, *Erythroxylum novogranatense* var. *truxillense* ("tupa"). Most coca today (*E. novogranatense* var. *novogranatense*, or "mamox") are grown on the eastern slopes of the Andes, though centuries ago the Incas also cultivated and consumed *tupa*, the western-slope variety (Rostworowski de Diez Canseco 1973). Because of its flavor and aroma, the tupa leaf was the variety chosen to be processed and added in an earlier, cocaine-laced concoction of Coca-Cola (Plowman 1979:111–114).

The uniqueness of each chaupiyunga or middle valley is the result of particular set of geological and geographical factors. In general, valleys in northern Peru have a more gradual slope than those of the south. Someone traveling in the Jequetepeque Valley in northern Peru can reach 2,200 meters above sea level (masl) by trekking 120 km, whereas in the Moquegua Valley in southern Peru the same altitude can be reached by walking only 80 km. Stephen Brush (1977:10–16) has suggested that such variations in the length and steepness of the valley result in different economic strategies: in flatter valleys with a gentler gradient, exchange or trade would be the dominant mode of exchange, but in steeper valleys, communities would opt for direct colonization.

More archaeological investigations have been carried out on the coast or in the highlands than in the chaupiyunga. Highland and coastal cities booming with business and tourism have become centers of archaeological projects. By contrast, small towns and villages of the middle valley often lack the infrastructure preferred by archaeologists—stores, shops, supermarkets, internet cafés—and as a result the prehistoric social systems of the chaupiyunga remain poorly understood. Frequently, when we speak of "coast-highland interaction," it is literally only the coastal and highland sites that we have data from. But the chaupiyunga, a nexus between different cultures and polities, must have played a crucial role in that interaction.

As early as the Preceramic Period, the middle valley had witnessed monumental construction in the form of large platform mounds (Burger 1992). By the end of the Initial Period, many more settlements were established at valley necks between the coastal plain and middle valley, a pattern suggesting communities vying for control of this important area of canal intake (Moseley 2001). Yoshio Onuki (1985) proposed that a distinct Yunga Tradition, with its settlement and subsistence systems adapted to local conditions, had already emerged before the arrival of pottery in the Central Andes.

Defensive structures like hilltop forts, ramparts, and ringworks appeared during the Initial Period in the valleys of Santa, Nepeña, and Casma. David Wilson (1988:323–324) believed that warfare at this time was between coastal valleys rather than between the coast and the highlands, though such early signs of warfare preluded an uneasy relationship between Moche states of the Santa-Nepeña-Casma complex and their highland, Recuay neighbors in the Callejón de Huaylas. Donald Proulx's survey of the Nepeña Valley shows two clearly separated clusters of settlements, one Moche and the other Recuay, in the chaupiyunga zone (Proulx 1982). A rare incidence of interethnic conflict was recorded in prehispanic Andean art: a Moche potter, who either saw or imagined his compatriots fighting Recuay warriors, painted the battle on a stirrup-spout bottle that is now in the collection of the Ethnologisches Museum in Berlin (Lau 2004).

Unlike the valleys of southern Peru, those in the north did not have any major Wari or Tiwanaku sites during the Middle Horizon. It is likely that the Wari did not conquer the north coast, but the constant association of Cajamarca pottery and *Spondylus* at Wari sites suggests that communities of northern Peru had nonetheless participated in the transportation of this spiny-shell oyster to highland empires of the south (T. Topic 1991:243; Tsai 2012a:48).

The rise of powerful maritime states like Sicán and Chimor brought the chaupiyunga, partially or wholly, into their sphere of control. In the Moche Valley, Theresa Topic (1990:183) recorded a boundary wall ("early-dating" Chimu) and hilltop lookouts ("later Chimu") at the confluence of Rio Moche and Rio La Cuesta; she suggested that this area was the border between the coast and the chaupiyunga. Archaeological surveys indicate the presence of coastal-style pottery and rectangular compounds in the Middle Jequetepeque Valley (Ravines 1982), and ethnohistorical documents mention alliance between coastal and highland polities of northern Peru (Cabello Valboa 1951 [1586]:317). Recent excavations conducted at the site of Collambay, directed by Alicia Boswell in the chaupiyunga zone of the Middle Moche Valley, revealed a cooperative relationship—possibly a political alliance—between Chimor and local mid-valley communities (Boswell 2016).

We know of at least two cases where the Incas exerted control over coca lands in the chaupiyunga: the Chillón and Moche Valleys. Tom Dillehay's pioneering archaeological work in the Middle Chillón Valley uncovered the Inca center of Huancayo Alto, which featured lower-class and elite residences, administrative complexes, drying terraces, and storage units (Dillehay 1976; 1977). In the Middle Moche Valley, colonial documents mentioned that two parcels of coca lands (Guancha and Yapon) belonged to the Inca king and another one (Arensa) was given to the Inca's mother (Netherly 1988:271). The Spanish Conquest resulted in an apocalyptic decline of population on the coast and in the chaupiyunga. Devastated by disease and political unrest, chaupiyunga communities also experienced forced relocations and encroachments of their land by Spanish settlers, and to these injustices they contested in court (Hart 1983:276). Such calamities, together with ecclesiastical efforts to eradicate coca and its associated cults, contributed to the disintegration of chaupiyunga culture and society.

Myth and Ethnicity in the Chaupiyunga: The Huarochirí Manuscript

The Huarochirí Manuscript is the only example we have of a book-length narrative written almost entirely in Quechua from the early colonial era. Currently archived in the National Library of Spain, the manuscript is part of a bundle of documents collected by Francisco de Avila (1573–1647), a Spanish curate who served in the province of Huarochirí in the highlands of Lima. In 1607, native parishioners filed complaints against Avila, alleging abuses. He was put in jail but was eventually cleared of those charges. A year later, Avila returned with a shock-and-awe campaign to destroy idolatry, his efforts culminating in a fiery auto-da-fé in the main plaza of Lima that treated onlookers to spectacles of mummy immolation and flagellation. Gerald Taylor (2008:9) suggested that Avila had prepared the Huarochirí Manuscript and orchestrated his crusade as a defense and counterattack against his accusers.

If true, the Huarochirí Manuscript would have been a self-dooming exegesis of indigenous beliefs that is unique for being written in a native Andean language, Quechua. The result of Avila's efforts is the textual preservation of the stories, customs, and beliefs of the Huarochirí people during the seventeenth century, including mythical accounts of highland-chaupiyunga interaction. The manuscript is an anonymous work, though Alan Durston (2007) has argued that it was written by Cristóbal Choquecasa, a native Checa leader whose handwriting on another document matches that of the Huarochirí Manuscript.

Avila's intent was to wipe out pagan belief, but the manuscript's narrator (Choquecasa?) wanted to keep his gods and ancestors in remembrance: "I set forth here the lives of the ancestors of the Huaro Cheri people, who all descend from one forefather: What faith they held, how they live up until now, those things and more; Village by village it will be written down: how they lived from their dawning age onward" (Huarochirí Manuscript 1991 [ca. 1608]:41–42). The Huarochirí Manuscript can be analyzed from multiple angles; much of its rich and complicated themes still awaits scholarly research. In this section, I focus on narratives concerning ethnic relations between yuncas (people living in the chaupiyunga zone) and highlanders and the rituals that mythologize their encounters.

Our starting anchor for understanding the Huarochirí myths is the narrator. He is from the highlands and a member of the Checa ethnic group. He extols the heroic ventures of highland *huacas* (powerful supernatural beings) in defeating and displacing the yuncas who now occupy the chaupiyunga and the coast. A central figure in these stories is the highland huaca of Pariacaca who, together with his children, battled the yunca people (Huarochirí Manuscript 1991 [ca. 1608]:70). Pariacaca's son, Tutay Quiri, transformed himself into yellow and red rain, charged down the Sici Caya and Mama (the Lurín and Rímac) Rivers, and pushed the yuncas into the middle valley and onto the coast.

Many yuncas were kicked out, but some stayed and submitted to Tutay Quiri and Pariacaca (Huarochirí Manuscript 1991 [ca. 1608]:71, 75–76, 80). Tutay Quiri told his new converts: "Stay here; you shall come to recognize my father [Pariacaca]. Living henceforth, address the Checa [highlanders] as 'brothers' and say, 'We're their brothers, the youngest ones.'" Thus the yuncas submitted to the invader's *huaca* and accepted a lower place in the genealogical order.

In another encounter, Pariacaca and his son Chuqui Huampo fought the female huaca Mana Ñamca, who lived below San Pedro de Mama in the chaupiyunga (Huarochirí Manuscript 1991 [ca. 1608]:69). In that battle, she broke Chuqui Huampo's foot, but Mana Ñamca was eventually defeated and cast into the ocean. Because of his injury, Chuqui Huampo had to stay behind and guard the valley in case Mana Ñamca came back. Pariacaca, worried about his son, told Chuqui Huampo that "all the inhabitants of these two valleys must give coca to you first, before any of them may chew it. Only after you have chewed it shall the people chew coca from their harvest." According to Avila's informants, Chuqui Huampo still sits in that spot, nursing his foot, watching the sea, and chewing the coca offered to him by yunca communities ("They carry on the custom secretly to this day").

Chapter 31 of the manuscript describes how Yasali, the child of a yunca man, was abandoned and orphaned when a group of highland marauders wearing stone helmets drove the yuncas out of Cocha (Huarochirí Manuscript 1991 [ca. 1608]:137). Llacsa Misa, the leader of the invaders, wanted to adopt Yasali, but Llacsa Misa's brothers wanted to kill the boy. "Better to let him live," said Llacsa Misa, defending the boy. "He'll show us all their customs, their fields, and everything" [causacochon caymi yma ayca causascantapa chacrantapas ymantaps aycantapas richuchi huasson]. So the boy was spared. Yasali grew up herding Llacsa Misa's llamas; later he married Llacsa Misa's sister and became a priest in the Uma Pacha festival.

The Uma Pacha festival, also called Chuta Cara, happened once a year. It alternated with the Machua festival every two years (Huarochirí Manuscript 1991 [ca. 1608]:121). Thus Uma Pacha (Year 1) → Uma Pacha (Year 2) → Machua (Year 3) → Machua (Year 4) → Uma Pacha (Year 5) → Uma Pacha (Year 6) → Machua (Year 7) → Machua (Year 8), and so on. These ceremonies consisted of huaca processions, llama sacrifice, dancing, and spear-throwing contests that used feathers ("tamta") to mark where the targets were hit.

The Machua festival, also called "Macua yunca," was performed by ayllus with yunca names. It is unclear, however, whether the performers were actual yuncas or were highlanders who inherited yunca names. Frank Salomon (Huarochirí Manuscript 1991 [ca. 1608]:123, footnote 652) interpreted the Machua festival as an allusion to Tamta Ñamca, a yunca lord whose house was decorated with feathers (Huarochirí Manuscript 1991 [ca. 1608]:55). A 1609 Jesuit report described the *Inaccha* ceremony where participants dressed "al modo yunga" and raced with colorful feathers (Arguedas and Duviols 1966:247). The feather, then, might have been a metonymic symbol of the yunca.

During Machua, people threw spears at two effigies that represented a man (Yomca) and a woman (Huasca). One ayllu would throw the spears first, followed by another ayllu, proceeding "ayllu by ayllu." The term "ayllu by ayllu" (ayllompi ayllompi, ayllo ayllomanta, etc.) appears four times in the manuscript (Huarochirí Manuscript 1991 [ca. 1608]:100, 102, 118, 122) and is always associated with worship or ceremony. This shows that macrogroups such as the Checas (checacuna) or yuncas (yuncacuna) were composed of ayllus that were listed and recognized during ritual. Rappaport would have recognized the sequential action of ayllus as an instantiation and validation of their existence, just like what Urton (1992) observed for the ayllus of Pacariqtambo when they gathered for communal work or celebration.

Each Huarochirí ayllu was divided into patrilineages or *yumay* (Huarochirí Manuscript 1991 [ca. 1608]:64 [F71V]). We can therefore distinguish three levels of group integration: the yumay (lineage), ayllu (community), and macrogroup (ethnic collective). The term "ayllu" is not precise, as it could also refer to the macrogroup or a village/settlement. Furthermore, ayllus from one macrogroup could break off and join another macrogroup (see Marcus 2000:238).

María Rostworowski de Diez Canseco (1978) argues that the stories in the manuscript reflect real instances of highlanders moving toward the coast during the Late Intermediate. Regardless of the truth or reality of these battles, the constant use of the term "yunca" or "yuncacuna" indicates the perception or conceptualization of a group of people: "All the Yunca shared one single way of life" [porque yuncacunaca huc causayniocllam tucoynin(pas) carcan] (Huarochirí Manuscript 1991 [ca. 1608]:71). On Folio 76R, the narrator, himself a highlander, imagined what the yunca would have thought about his people: "And the Yunca, speaking for themselves, say 'the highlanders [sallcacuna] are getting along all right. It's because they carry on our old way of life that their people flourish so'" (Huarochirí Manuscript 1991 [ca. 1608]:76). This is a remarkable passage. Not only is the narrator aware of an ethnic "other," but he then also proceeds to project his own ethnic awareness onto the yunca other! As a final warning, the narrator emphasizes the importance of ritual in keeping an ethnic group alive: "The Yunca don't practice [Pariacaca worship] anymore. . . . It's because of that fault of theirs that the Yunca are becoming extinct." Indeed, I make a similar argument in chapter 5.

Following defeat in battle, a yunca could be incorporated into Pariacaca's cult, showing the fluidity of membership: by changing one's huaca, a yunca could become ritually and genealogically integrated into another group. The Uma Pacha and Machua evoked the coexistence and ritual integration of yuncas and highlanders, transgressing and yet still preserving ethnic boundaries, encapsulating Barthian principles described in chapter 1. The cycling of Machua and Uma Pacha and the spear-throwing contest by ayllus are examples of Rappaport's "discrete categorization" and "self-reference." People could change identities—Yasali was a yunca later turned Concha—but discrete ethnic categories continued to be preserved in myths and ceremonies.

The Huarochirí Manuscript can be seen as a mythological map of the social and ritual landscape. In this map, ayllus and huacas were connected to each other through narratives about their life, exploits, and movement. Their positions were not absolute but relative. Because of their defeat in supernatural battles, the yunca were a people living at an altitude lower than the Checas, and, once incorporated, occupy a lower rung in the social hierarchy. If we follow the manuscript literally, it would appear that at one time the yunca were the original inhabitants of the highlands (Huarochirí Manuscript 1991 [ca. 1608]:66), but because of their displacement by the followers of Pariacaca, they now occupy the warm middle valley. Again, the ethnic descriptor "yunca" denotes a position *relative* to the narrator and not an absolute, fixed place.

The Huarochirí stories, then, illustrate the nonlinear nature of Andean narratives, where plots and characters do not form neat sequential developments. Events fold onto and interweave with each other. Causation sometimes runs backward, as if heros and huacas can jump into a time machine to alter the past by going into the future. Unaccustomed to such disregard for Western spatial-temporal order, the editor of the manuscript (Avila?), desperately trying to make heads or tails of the sequence of events, heavily annotated the page margins with questions like "ask who was born before" or "ask where this mountain is" or "ask whether he is the son or brother." But the Huarochirí narrative is not history, or story, but a map. As Michael Moseley (2001:51) notes, "This all-encompassing cosmology provides deep identification with the environment. Andean people literally read their physical surroundings as a resonant text of sacred places and spaces that commemorate a trip across time and changing landscapes from super beings to human beings to present beings." But in the minds of Andean storytellers and listeners, no fundamental difference comes between past and present times, and a normal being is always on the verge of becoming something super.

Ethnic Conflicts in Quivi, Middle Chillón Valley

Ethnicity under Empire

> There is a Socratic parable, well known in some quarters, about a teacher who gives his students two magnifying glasses and invites them to look at the one through the other. When each has told of all he has learned, the sage delivers his lesson in the form of a question, a *coup de grace*: "Of what have you told me," he asks, "the thing you have seen or the thing through which you have seen it?"
> —John Comaroff (1987:301)

The stories contained in the Huarochirí Manuscript were local and provincial, recounting the battles and rituals between neighboring ethnic groups. Chronicles of the Inca Empire, by contrast, concerned the vast territory of the Andes, which contained a multitude of languages and ethnic groups. Rather than being described by a relative position to the speaker ("she is a yunga"), ethnic groups under the empire were assigned specific names associated with a curaca, capac, or polity ("she is Chimo"). This specificity of ethnic names no doubt reflected the concern of imperial administrators to track their subjects. The magnifying glasses mentioned in the Socratic parable, through which we will now view the case of ethnic conflicts in Quivi, are the lenses of empire.

When Cieza de León describes the cultural diversity of Inca Cuzco, he starts reciting the names of various ethnic groups:

> As the city was full of foreign nationals and pilgrims, Indians of Chile, Pasto, Cañaris, Chachapoyas, Huancas, and Collas were there in the place and part that were indicated by the governors of the city. They kept the costumes of their fathers, and went about using the costumes in the way they were used in their native land; and although together there were one hundred thousand men, they easily recognized each other by the insignias they put on their heads. (Cieza de León 1984 [1553]:118; my translation)

> those of each nation will speak their own language, throughout all this kingdom they all wore special insignia on their head to distinguish themselves one from the other. If they were Yungas, they went muffled like gypsies; if Collas, they wore caps shaped like mortars, of wool; if Canas, they wore larger caps, and much broader. The Cañari wore a kind of narrow wooden crown like the rim of a sieve; the Huancas, strands that fell below their chin, and their hair braided; the Canchis, broad black or red bands over their forehead. Thus all of them could be recognized by their insignia, which was such a good and clear system that even if there were five hundred thousand men together, they could be clearly told from each other. (Cieza de León 1959 [1553]:71)

Such division along ethnic lines, Cobo (1979 [1653]:195–197) explains, was necessary to recognizing "who were the most diligent in serving [the Inca] on the occasions that came up in peace and war" and thus creating an atmosphere of competition between groups. The dress code allowed ethnic lords to monitor their people's movement:

> The vassals were not permitted to move from one province to another on their own free will. In fact, all vassals had to reside in their towns; they could

> not leave or wander around or take trips through strange lands without permission from their caciques. The men and women of each nation and province had their insignias and emblems by which they could be identified, and they could not go around without this identification or exchange their insignias for those of another nation, or they would be severely punished. (Cobo 1979 [1653]:196)

> One thing is very noticeable, that, although the clothing and costume of the Indians is simple, still all the provinces are differentiated, especially by what they wear on their heads. . . . And it was an inviolable law that no one might change the costume and habit of province even though he moved to another, and the Inca considered this very important to good government. (Acosta 2002 [1590]:356)

In an empire where laborers were constantly relocated from one province to another, mandatory clothing and insignia became a kind of ID that allowed administrators to accurately gauge the number and distribution of tribute payers.

Canta vs. Chaclla

In resolving community disputes, colonial arbitrators often favored one party over another. The enforced ceasefire between ethnic groups, like the lid of a pressure cooker, was lifted after the collapse of Tawantinsuyu. Rekindling old rivalries and stirring vigilante violence, native leaders soon learned that battles in the lettered mountains of Peru would be settled not by warriors but by lawyers.

The Canta and the Chaclla, two groups native to the highlands of Lima, fought over chaupiyunga land in the valley of Chillón, first through traditional tooth and nail and later through litigations (1558–1570). (Court documents from this case, archived as Justicia 413 in the Archivo General de Indias in Seville, are now viewable online at http://pares.mcu.es.) In pre-Inca times, the Canta invaded the middle valley and claimed rights to the territories of Quivi, a chaupiyunga group allied with the coastal kingdom of Collec, or Colli. The Inca Empire, after conquering the Chillón Valley, placed Chaclla *mitmaqs* (colonists whose settlement was mandated by the Inca Empire) in the chaupiyunga zone once controlled by the Quivi (Rostworowski de Diez Canseco 1988:61–62). Here is a quick dramatis personae, in case one is already confused: Canta (highland), Chaclla (highland), Quivi (chaupiyunga), and Colli (coast).

After the Spanish conquest, the Canta and the Chaclla began fighting over the land around the Quivi. During the Great Inca Revolt waged by Manco Inca against Spanish rule (1536), the Canta joined Inca rebels, while the Chaclla refused to take part. The Chaclla and Canta continued their feud during this time of chaos. The Canta tricked a Chaclla curaca into a meeting where they killed him and his followers.

In 1549, Francisco de Ampuero and Nicolás de Ribera, Spanish encomenderos in charge of the Canta and Chaclla, tried to end this conflict by making the Canta pay 200 "obejas [ovejas] de la tierra" (llamas or alpacas) to the Chaclla as compensation for the chaupiyunga lands. The Chaclla refused to accept the animals and, dissatisfied with the arrangement, filed suit on October 5, 1558. Throughout the litigation, the Canta and Chaclla went on damaging each other's irrigation canals, boundary markers, and coca plants. The court in Lima ultimately ruled in favor of the Chaclla, a decision consistent with the colonial policy of keeping the status quo of Inca mitmaq settlement (Rostworowski de Diez Canseco 1988:67).

This episode of the Chaclla-Canta feud illustrates the influence of empire in not only regulating but also forming and shaping ethnic groups. First, what does it mean when we say *the* Chaclla, *the* Quivi, or *the* Canta? Under Inca rule, the Chaclla was an amalgam of three administrative units (*waranqas*): Chaclla, Carampoma, and Casta (Spalding 1984:Figure 1). Each waranqa was a unit of about 1,000 tribute-paying families; the waranqa was divided into 10 *pachakas*, units of 100 tribute-paying families. Inca administrative units, however, did not necessarily coincide with indigenous sociopolitical units. This decimally nested hierarchy with clear divisions between units was an administrative ideal enforced by the Inca Empire, and when such hierarchies were not present, the empire would create new groups or change the composition of existing ones (C. Julien 1982).

It is unclear how distinct each waranqa was culturally or linguistically. On the coast, there were two groups that spoke different languages: Carabayllo and Pachacamac (Marcus and Silva 1988:18). We could imagine, then, that the highland waranqas were different culturally from the yunga waranqas. In the Middle Chillón Valley, there were many chaupiyunga waranqas including the Quivi, Guancayo, Guaravi, Maca, and Sapán, with each waranqa occupying only one side of the river. Archaeologically, we might find that the pottery style of the chaupiyunga, as a whole, was different from that of the highlands, but we could be amiss in attempting to distinguish one chaupiyunga waranqa from another.

The Middle Chillón Valley episode gained fame as the third case of Murra's vertical archipelago (see chapter 3). Murra (1972) hypothesizes that the coastal kingdom of Colli had placed colonists within Quivi (chaupiyunga) territory. Santoro et al. (2010) combine archaeological, ethnohistorical, and bioanthropological data to suggest that multiple modes of exchange and migration—colonization, trade, intermarriage, military outpost—were practiced in the middle valley. Rostworowski de Diez Canseco's (1977) review of the Justicia 413 document reveals an interesting arrangement in which highlanders descended to the chaupiyunga to help local farmers with their harvest. In return, these highlanders received some of the harvested crops or produce, including cotton and coca.

The complexity of the relationships between groups of the chaupiyunga must have dismayed Spanish judges. It is not a simple dichotomy of highlanders versus the yungas; instead, many groups were involved, with alliances made between yungas and highlanders. Don Luis Zacalla Chunbi, the leader of the chaupiyunga village of Guarabi, stated that "with the Indians of Canta he has a great friendship, and they are partners because he deals with them, selling the coca in exchange for llama and potatoes" (Marcus and Silva 1988:30). During an episode of drought in the middle valley, the Canta, together with the Quivi, built canals that carried water from higher-elevation lakes (Rostworowski de Diez Canseco 1988:61; Justicia 413:folio 206r). It was a cooperative relationship, though not an unselfish one: the Quivi paid tribute to the Canta, and any investment in the Quivi's hydraulic infrastructure would ensure more revenues in the form of coca back to the Canta. Thus ethnic groups in their history of interaction wavered between being friends and being enemies—they were "frenemies" who strategically made or broke alliances.

To Rule Is to Classify

> Is [ethnicity] an object of analysis, something to be explained?
> Or is it an explanatory principle capable of illuminating
> significant aspects of human existence? Does it really refer to
> "idols of the tribe," or is it in fact an idol of the scribe?
> —John Comaroff (1987:301)

The classification of Andean societies was an administrative exercise for empires. Shortly after their arrival in the Americas, Spanish conquerors and administrators noticed the relationship between indigenous environment, culture, and society. Those seeking a fortune realized that a productive, fertile region could support a large native workforce from which one could demand tribute, derive profit, and attain wealth. Certain environments were apparently easier to administer, a pattern noted by Cieza de León, who hypothesized that restricted or circumscribed environments led to docile subjects: "Those from Peru serve well and are tame . . . because they were subjects of the Inca kings. . . . In this condition they were born; and if they did not want to do so, they were constrained by necessity, for the land of Peru is barren, full of mountains and snowy fields. If they were to leave their villages and valleys to these deserts, they could not live, for the land does not give fruit. . . . In order to live and not die they have to serve and not abandon their lands" (Cieza de León 2000 [1553]:105–106, my translation). Cieza's writing was cited by Herbert Spencer in his *Principles of Sociology*, and Spencer's ideas in turn influenced Robert Carneiro's circumscription theory of state origin (Carneiro 1981:180–181, footnote 131).

Andean societies were thus ranked under the logic of empire: the savage and barbarous were impossible to conquer, but foreign kingdoms proved easier to subdue and plunder. So now we have an answer to Comaroff's question regarding the lens through which we see ethnicity: for archaeologists studying ethnicity in prehistory, it is the layers of historical empires that could distort our vision. Not only did the rise and collapse of empires affect the dynamics of contemporaneous ethnic groups, but empires, in the very long run, leave a legacy of self-awareness, a slew of history-changing that obscures our understanding of how non-state societies recognize cultural difference. It might mislead us into thinking that these societies shared the same ethnocentrism as nation-states. It might make us believe that all societies would divide peoples, like colonial administrators, into neat and clear categories. With all its defects and inadequacies, we still need the help of archaeology to show us how aboriginal ethnic groups interact without the empire's meddling.

3

Las Varas

A Community in the Jequetepeque Valley

A kingdom that . . . was cunningly concealed, tucked into a valley amongst mountains, entrance to which could be gained only by one pass not easily found, and before this pass was a rushing river over which was but one bridge, the narrowest in the world.
—Thomas Berger, *Arthur Rex*, 158

Archaeologists investigating ethnic interaction in the Chillón Valley or the Huarochirí area have benefited from a rich corpus of colonial-era texts, but we do not have such detailed records, transcribed and published, from the mid-valley Jequetepeque, though these documents might someday be found in the regional archives of La Libertad (Trujillo), San Pedro de Lloc, or Cajamarca. This is a future task for historians and anthropologists interested in complementing a burgeoning "chaupiyunga archaeology" with archival data.

In this and the following chapters, I focus on one particular chaupiyunga village, Las Varas, founded in the Jequetepeque Valley around AD 1000 (Figure 3.1). I begin with a description of the environmental setting of the Middle Jequetepeque Valley, a chaupiyunga zone trafficked by migrants and caravans who made their journey along the river and *quebradas*, lateral ravines that deviate from the main valley. A thousand years ago, this was a crossroads of cultures and polities, such as those labeled by archaeologists as Cajamarca and Lambayeque. Here we find Las Varas, a village built on a patch of land physically cut off from neighboring settlements, "cunningly concealed [and] tucked into a valley amongst mountains." This archaeological site proved to be an ideal laboratory to test Murra's hypothesis regarding the presence of a transplanted colony, or what he called the "vertical archipelago," on the north coast of Peru. The chapter concludes with a presentation of my research design for testing models of trade and colonization utilizing excavation data from Las Varas.

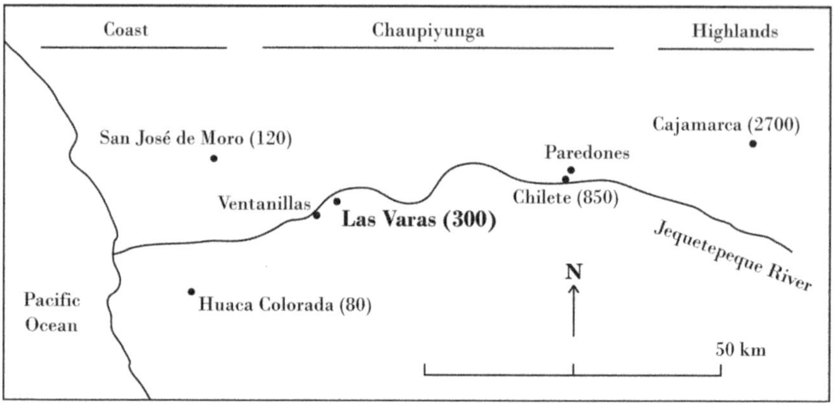

Figure 3.1. Map of the Jequetepeque Valley. Numbers in parentheses indicate elevation (meters above sea level). (Courtesy of Howard Tsai)

Quebradas in the Middle Jequetepeque Valley

The Andean Cordillera upon reaching northern Peru veers away from the coast and leaves in its wake ever-larger farmlands of rice, maize, and sugarcane. The three largest valleys of the north coast are the Chicama, Jequetepeque, and Lambayeque, breadbaskets of coastal states and kingdoms like the Moche, Chimu, and Sican. The Lambayeque system, the largest of the three, is actually a conglomerate of smaller rivers like La Leche, Reque, and Lambayeque.

The Jequetepeque Valley, south of Lambayeque and north of Chicama, has both abundant agricultural fields and water flow. The Oficina Nacional de Evaluación de Recursos Naturales (ONERN) (1988:14) divides the Jequetepeque Valley into lower (0–225 masl), middle (225–600 masl), and upper sectors (600–4,183 masl). The lower valley, or the coast, receives 15.6–31.2 mm of precipitation annually (ONERN 1988:16). Modern farmers cultivate rice in one season (December–May) and maize in the other (June–November).

The middle valley is sunny and warm. Flourishing along riverbanks are mango and algarrobo trees (*Prosopis* sp.), acacia (also faique, *Acacia macracantha*), and stalks of bamboo-like cane (caña brava, *Gynerium sagittatum*). Dotted on the rocky hillside away from the river are fruit-bearing sapote shrubs (*Capparis angulata*) and columns of cacti (*Cereus macrostibas*) standing like sentries. This ecological zone, the chaupiyunga, is suitable for growing coca. Modern coca fields in the region of La Libertad are restricted to the Upper Chicama Valley, but colonial documents mention coca fields in the Upper Moche as well (Netherly 1988:270).

During my survey of the Jequetepeque Valley in 2005, I was struck by the constant association of quebradas—dry ravines that branch off from the main river—with archaeological features such as walls, structures, and petroglyphs. Prehispanic compounds are frequently found next to the quebrada's entrance. Quebrada intersections, strategically important for travel and communication, may also have been ritually significant. Contemporary Andean communities make offerings and sacrifices at the confluence of two rivers, an act that expresses the concept of *tinkuy*, which means "coming-together" in Quechua (Allen 1988: 65; Arriaga 1968 [1621]:48; Bauer 1998:118–119; Mayer 1977:76–78; Murra 1980:14). Indeed, located at the tinkuy of the Jequetepeque River and the Quebrada Chausís is the site of Yonán, a unique local landmark famed for its vast spread of petroglyphs carved on boulders and cliffsides (Pimentel 1986:24–25, 121–143).

Many mid-valley quebradas serve as natural routes to the highlands. Sometimes they connect one valley to another, like the Quebrada Montegrande near Tembladera, which links the Jequetepeque with the Chamán to the north. Today, the larger quebradas are traveled infrequently by *combis* (small vans) that go from one remote town to another, but caveat emptor: the driver does not guarantee when, if ever, the passenger will get a return ride.

The smaller quebradas lack paved roads and are used only by farmers and herders. The Quebrada del Caracol, located behind Las Varas, is utilized yearround by cattle herders, but because of its remoteness, many residents of Pay Pay are unaware of its existence. Herbert Eling (1987:371) noted the use of this quebrada as a route connecting Ventanillas in the middle valley to the highlands of Trinidad. In 2007, I trekked into this quebrada with herders from Pay Pay who kept their cattle there. They were to meet and pay the *comuneros* (community members) of Trinidad who owned the quebrada. At this meeting or "rodeo," those from Pay Pay counted their livestock corralled in the quebrada, haggled with the comuneros over the mandatory fee, and finally coughed up the payment. The meeting point was quite deep into the quebrada, and here, some three hours of hike from Las Varas, I found prehispanic structures and petroglyphs, one of which depicted a condor hovering above a double-headed serpent. The ritual plazas of Las Varas were built next to the entrance to this quebrada, thereby connecting the chaupiyunga with the highlands of Trinidad and Contumazá (chapter 5).

Books on the Inca Empire often depict Inca road systems as a ladder running along the spine of the Andes: one rail on the coast and the other in the highlands, with rungs in the valleys that connect the coast to the highlands. The presence of human activity in the quebradas, however, shows that coast-highland traffic is in fact much more complex. Not only did we encounter sites on both banks of the river, but we also found sites in the quebradas and their branches, with artifacts and structures appearing in even smaller ravines that deviate from the major quebrada. Archaeologists who specialize in survey (e.g., Parsons 2009) will no doubt delight in exploring these quebradas of the chaupiyunga, which are like hallways filled with corridors that still contain unrecorded sites (see Wilson 1988:24–25 for similar findings in the Santa Valley).

Lambayeque, Chimu, and Cajamarca: Cultural Interactions in the Jequetepeque Valley

Radiocarbon dates from Las Varas place the site's occupation at around AD 1000 (see chapter 4), right on the dividing line between the Middle Horizon (AD 600–1000) and Late Intermediate (AD 1000–1460). The Middle Horizon is stereotypically portrayed as a time of political unity and high civilization, whereas the Late Intermediate evokes images of an Andean "dark age" characterized by chaos and balkanization. This perspective might be true for certain regions like the highlands of central and southern Peru, but the exact opposite better describes the north coast where the Moche collapsed during the Middle Horizon, and only later, during the Late Intermediate, did coastal states resurrect and an empire emerge.

The Lower Jequetepeque Valley during the Middle Horizon was a fragmented landscape filled with competing Mochica polities (Dillehay et al. 2009; Swenson 2006). The leaders of these balkanized fiefdoms ruled from hilltop fortresses and temples, utilizing both war and worship as extensions of Moche politics. Ceramic artisans at San José de Moro produced vessels whose surface was jampacked with drawings of mythical figures and arabesque designs. Given their talent and artistry, Moche potters of Moro must have appreciated the exotic, colorful bottles and bowls coming from Cajamarca, Wari, and the central coast of Peru, tradewares later discovered by archaeologists in Late Moche burials (Castillo 2001; McClelland et al. 2007).

Most archaeologists assumed that Moche warfare was conducted between Moche combatants, that is, those sharing a common Moche culture, but Marco Rosas Rintel argues that, based on his discovery of Cajamarca-style fineware in the elite residences of Cerro Chepén, highlanders from Cajamarca invaded the lower valley and contributed to the collapse of the Moche culture (Rosas Rintel 2007). Cajamarca-style pottery is also ubiquitous in other Late Moche sites of the Jequetepeque Valley, including Cerro Chepén (Rosas Rintel 2007), Huaca Colorada (Swenson et al. 2011:123), and San José de Moro (Bernuy and Bernal 2008). I should caution that pottery, especially fineware, might alternatively indicate trade and/or intermarriage rather than conquest; indeed Rosas Rintel had included architectural evidence to bolster his argument.

On the north coast, the most prolific huaca-building kingdom at the start of the Late Intermediate was Sican. Its capital, the archaeological site of Batan Grande, had been founded in an algarrobo forest in the La Leche Valley. Ten massive huacas, sandy-brown icebergs floating above a sea of algarrobo trees, were constructed between AD 900 and 1100 (Middle Sican period). The Sican polity was part (if not the epicenter) of a larger cultural phenomenon known as "Lambayeque" that promulgated single-spout ceramic bottles and gold masks depicting an individual with upturned almond-shaped eyes and pointy ears. This person has several names given by archaeologists, including Sican Lord, Sican Deity, and Huaco Rey (Shimada 1981; 1990).

The Lambayeque archaeological culture had spread south to the Jequetepeque Valley. Luis Jaime Castillo (2001:327–328) argues that Lambayeque polities conquered the Jequetepeque Valley at the beginning of the Late Intermediate, though some scholars believed that the valley had maintained its independence until the Chimu Conquest (Shimada 1990:339; Sapp 2011:102; Swenson 2004: 339). Lambayeque-style pottery was prevalent in the Jequetepeque Valley, but the architectural layout of local sites (such as Pacatnamu and Cabur) differed from that of Sican, Túcume, and other sites from the Lambayeque area (Sapp 2002:75–76). Late Intermediate adobes of the Jequetepeque Valley lacked makers' marks (D. H. McClelland 1986:39; Prieto Burmester 2010:239; Tsai 2012b), unlike adobes from contemporary sites in the Lambayeque region (Shimada 1997:77–83). In sum, the Lambayeque style in the Jequetepeque Valley displayed influences from the north but eventually developed its own distinctive, local elements (Sapp 2011).

The largest and most impressive Lambayeque-period site in the Jequetepeque Valley was Pacatnamu, a seaside sprawl of adobe compounds and pyramids next to the mouth of the river. Steep bluffs protected the site's southern and western flanks, while the northeast side was defended by three rings of massive city walls, the outermost wall being unfinished (Donnan 1986a). The core of Pacatnamu consisted of numerous rectangular compounds, cemeteries, and adobe pyramids, the largest of which was Huaca 1, measuring 70 × 70 m and more than 10 m high. Huaca 1 overlooked a rectangular compound, the Major Quadrangle, which Christopher Donnan (1986b:65, 80) interpreted as the residence of elite individuals.

Another major Lambayeque center was Ventanillas. Located 37 km from the coast at 280 masl (just 4 km west of Las Varas), Ventanillas is the easternmost adobe huaca in the Jequetepeque Valley. The site has recently been excavated by Robyn Cutright of Centre College (Cutright and Osores Mendives 2021). Its largest pyramid, named Ventanillas 1 (Reindel 1993) or Huaca 1 (Cutright 2013), measures 50 × 65 m and 12 m high (Reindel 1993:416). This massive huaca is characterized by chamber-and-fill construction with side ramps leading to the summit. Its adobes resemble Donald H. McClelland's (1986:28–29) "Intermediate" type with sharp edges and slightly concave surfaces. Judging from these architectural features, I had estimated that Huaca 1 was built sometime between AD 1000 and 1200 (Tsai 2012b:54), though recent radiocarbon samples from Ventanillas obtained by Cutright date to ca. 1200–1300 (Cutright and Osores Mendives 2021).

Herbert Eling (1987:416) has noted Coastal Cajamarca pottery at Ventanillas, and while my survey has confirmed his observation, the vast majority of the pottery I observed at Ventanillas is still Lambayeque or coastal in style (carinated and paddle-stamped ollas). Cutright's recent excavations have verified that coastal-style pottery is indeed the dominant ceramic assemblage at Ventanillas; only a small percentage (2–3%) of diagnostic sherds are in the Coastal Cajamarca style (Cutright and Osores Mendives 2021). By contrast 37% of diagnostic sherds from Las Varas are in the Coastal Cajamarca style (to be discussed in chapter 4). What was the relationship between coastal Pacatnamu and mid-valley Ventanillas? Perhaps these two centers were major players in the traffic of goods and resources in the valley during the Late Intermediate. Future excavations by Cutright will give us better insights into the nature of exchange and interaction between coastal Lambayeque communities and Ventanillas, a powerful center in the chaupiyunga zone.

During the second half of the Late Intermediate, Pacatnamu faced its greatest rival from the south—the maritime empire of Chimor or Chimu from the Moche Valley. Archaeologists refer to Chimor's capital as Chan Chan, though during colonial times a particular huaca within the area was called "Yomayoguan" (Ramírez 1996:123). At its height, Chan Chan was one of the largest prehispanic cities of the Andes, with 30,000–40,000 inhabitants living within an area of 20 km^2 (Moore and Mackey 2008:784). From here the rulers of Chimor, enshrined and entombed in their palaces, plotted their conquest of the coastal plains of Peru.

Scholars had previously placed the Chimu Conquest of the Jequetepeque Valley at around AD 1200, but Donnan (1986c:22) and Carol Mackey (2006:323; also Moore and Mackey 2008:789) suggested that the incursion happened around AD 1310. Spanish chronicler Antonio de la Calancha (1977 [1639]:1227) describes how the "Chimo Capac," the king of Chimor, sent a "brave captain" named Pacatnamu to conquer the Pacasmayo (Jequetepeque) Valley. Chimo Capac rewarded this victorious captain with a palace and governorship of the newly acquired province. Archaeologist Richard Keatinge (1982:207–208) identified this palace as the site of Farfán, later excavated by Keatinge and Conrad (1983) and Mackey (2001, 2004, 2012).

Located 13 km from the shore, Farfán consists of six rectangular compounds built beside the hills of Faclo. The site was in fact occupied during Lambayeque (pre-Chimu) times, since Mackey's excavations showed that Compound III of Farfán had been a Lambayeque structure that was later destroyed by the Chimu. Compounds II and VI, built under Chimu rule, resembled the palaces or *ciudadelas* of Chan Chan (Mackey 2009:330). Keatinge and Conrad had suggested that Compound II was the actual palace of that "brave captain" of Chimor. One of Mackey's most significant findings is the large-scale reuse and modification of Farfán during Inca times, a fascinating process not mentioned by the chroniclers. With its long history of occupation by multiple polities, Mackey's work at Farfán represents one of the best case studies of using archaeology to corroborate and correct a Spanish account that contains the semi-mythical past of a major coastal culture.

Compared to the coast, very few Late Intermediate sites have been excavated in the Middle Jequetepeque Valley; the most intensive mid-valley excavations were conducted in 1980–1981 by Rogger Ravines (1982) as part of the Gallito Ciego Dam rescue project (Keatinge 1980). Ravines (1982:158–164) excavated tripartite rectangular compounds with Late Intermediate pottery, which might suggest Chimu administration of the middle valley. Other evidence for Chimu occupation, such as audiencias and clusters of storerooms, is lacking.

According to the sixteenth-century Spanish chronicler Cabello Valboa (1951 [1586]:317), Chimor formed an alliance with its highland neighbor, Cajamarca, to resist the Inca Conquest (ca. AD 1460). Cabello's brief account sparked many speculations with regard to the relationship between the north coast and the highlands during the Late Intermediate, but we still do not know much about the political organization of the societies and communities of Cajamarca. Archaeological survey by Daniel Julien (1988; 1993) revealed that the three largest Cajamarca sites of the Late Intermediate were Santa Delia, Tantarica, and Guzmango Viejo. Interestingly, only Santa Delia is to be found in the Cajamarca Basin (Watanabe 2009) near the modern city of Cajamarca. The other two sites—Tantarica (Watanabe 2002) and Guzmango Viejo (Jaeckel and Melly Cava 1987)—are located south of the Jequetepeque River in the Contumazá area.

D. Julien (1993), by combining archaeological survey and Spanish census data (1572), argues that Cajamarca on the eve of the Inca invasion did not form a single kingdom or empire; the various waranqas (Inca administrative units of 1,000 tribute-paying households each) likely represented small polities or chiefdoms. Jason Toohey (2011) made a similar argument based on his analysis of the diversity of Cajamarca pottery from the fortified site of Yanaorco. Watanabe (2015:179–183) found various fragments (exact number unspecified) of Chimu pottery in Tantarica, whereas Toohey (2011:196) found only *one* possible coastal-style sherd—out of a total of 1,430 diagnostic sherds—at Yanaorco. I suspect that Cajamarca sites north of the Jequetepeque River, including the Cajamarca Basin, had limited interaction or contact with coastal states and empires during the Late Intermediate. By contrast, Cajamarca sites south of the Jequetepeque River, such as Tantarica and Guzmango in Contumazá that were closer to the Chimu capital, must have had greater interaction with Chimor. Indeed in Cabello's account, the lord of Cajamarca was named "Guzmango Capac," and in the 1572 *visita* or census of Cajamarca, the highest-ranking curaca, the overseer of all tribute-paying subjects in the Cajamarca region, was the lord of Guzmango from Contumazá.

Murra's Fourth Case

In Murra's seminal article (1972) on vertical archipelagos in the Andes, he presented the interaction between Chimu and Cajamarca as one of his five case studies. Murra suggested the possibility of highland (Cajamarca) and coastal (Chimu) colonies crisscrossing each other's territories, that is, Cajamarca colonists living within the Chimu domain, and vice versa. While admitting the speculative nature of his model, he encouraged archaeologists to look for these hypothetical colonies in their research. Archaeologist David Wilson (1999:303) took up the challenge but concluded that Murra's fourth case of Chimu-Cajamarca archipelagos lacked sufficient archaeological evidence. Investigations in the Moquegua area were able to document Wari and Tiwanaku colonists in coastal valleys (Goldstein 2005; Williams 2001), yet no prehispanic highland colony had been found on the north coast of Peru, nor coastal colonies in the highlands.

My 2005 survey of the Middle Jequetepeque Valley provided a possible candidate for Murra's elusive Chimu-Cajamarca archipelagos. The vast majority of archaeological research in northern Peru had concentrated on either the coast or the highlands, with very few projects focusing on the intervening area, the chaupiyunga or middle valley. To investigate the interaction between the coast and the highlands of northern Peru, I surveyed the Middle Jequetepeque Valley and excavated Las Varas. One goal was to test whether Las Varas was a highland colony—Murra's "vertical archipelago"—placed in the chaupiyunga zone between Chimor and Cajamarca.

Murra's fourth case is especially important since Rostworowski de Diez Canseco (1977) argues that coastal kingdoms had an economy different from that of highland hegemons like the Incas. Lords of the Peruvian coast sponsored specialists dedicated to full-time production of textiles, chicha, precious metal, and pottery. These specialists supplied their patrons with finished products in addition to trading among themselves, and archaeological research on the coast yielded corroborating evidence for this kind of specialization (Marcus 1987;

2008b; J. Topic 1990). The coastal-specialist model differed significantly from the highland-archipelago model, and debates over whether Andean societies were specialized or self-sufficient dominated discussions of prehispanic Andean economy.

Enrique Mayer (2002:58) notes that "no economic system is as pure as the models that scholars construct for it." So if a spectrum of economic strategies—ranging from self-sufficiency to specialization—existed in the Andes, how would different systems (specialized vs. autonomous) interact? Would highlanders ignore coastal people by setting up their own colonies, or would they exchange some of their products with coastal communities? Would some products be made locally, and others traded or imported? Most importantly, how can we as archaeologists investigate this problem using survey and excavation data?

A Test of Murra's Fourth Case at Las Varas

Archaeologist Charles Stanish (1992:41–48) listed the archaeological criteria for identifying a colony—the kind we would expect to qualify as Murra's archipelago. These criteria include (1) the colony having domestic artifacts and features (houses, cookware) imitating, in style, artifacts from the distant homeland; (2) the colony being surrounded by sites with artifacts made in the "indigenous" style that reflects local customs and practices; (3) a sudden, rather than gradual, appearance of "colonial" artifacts in the colony; and (4) control of a separate agricultural area by the colony (Stanish 1992:41–48).

Stanish's criteria are explicit, sound, and operational (testable using archaeological data), and therefore I decided to apply his research design to my study of coast-highland interaction in the Middle Jequetepeque Valley. In 2005, I conducted a survey of the lower Middle Jequetepeque Valley, starting from the valley neck near Talambo (150 masl) and ending near Tembladera by the Gallito Ciego Dam (400 masl). In this 30-km transect, almost all Late Intermediate sites had surface scatters of coastal-style domestic pottery characterized by carinated rims and paddle-stamped surfaces. One site, however, was unique in having large quantities of painted "Coastal Cajamarca" style of bowls. This site—Las Varas—had a ceramic assemblage in which Coastal Cajamarca pottery was the vast majority; no site in my survey had such a high proportion of Coastal Cajamarca sherds.

Las Varas, located in the Middle Jequetepeque Valley of northern Peru, is situated 40 km inland from the Pacific shore at an elevation of 300 masl (Figure 3.1). It sits on a patch of land, shaped like a half moon, on the south bank of the river (Figure 3.2). This area is physically cut off from neighboring settlements by the river and rice fields to the north and by steep cliffs to the east, west, and south. These natural barriers have turned Las Varas into a veritable island in

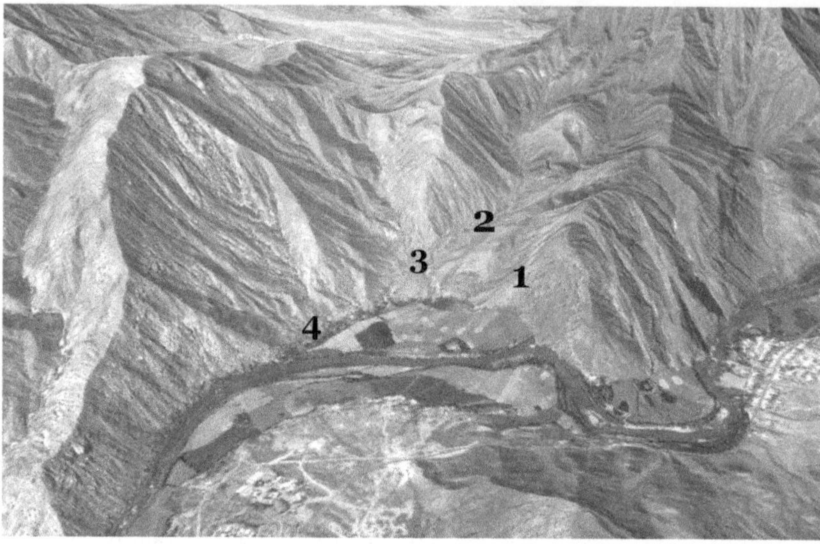

Figure 3.2. Google Earth image of Las Varas, looking south. Numbers indicate archaeological sectors within the site. The distance between Sectors 1 and 4 is approximately 1 km. (Map data: Google, Maxar Technologies, CNES/Airbus) (Courtesy of Howard Tsai)

the valley. The site covers a 50-ha area in which archaeological remains such as houses and burials are sparsely distributed rather than densely concentrated, so that ancient Las Varas was more like a village than a town. Two bridges connect Las Varas to modern settlements on the north bank: a large bridge in Gallito and a smaller suspension bridge in Pay Pay (Figure 3.3). During the dry months of July and August, someone from Gallito can walk on the exposed river cobbles and cross over to the other bank.

Within Las Varas, archaeological remains are concentrated in four sectors (Figure 3.4). Sector 1 is a terraced area littered with Coastal Cajamarca painted bowls and plain pottery made in the Cajamarca style. D. Julien (1988:132–133) has reported such terraces in the Cajamarca area, and he interprets them as "support for structures." My excavations at Las Varas have confirmed the terrace's function as support for residential structures or houses. Sector 2 consists of several standing stones about 30–40 cm tall arranged to form a circle; I counted approximately 30 such circular features. Since the center of these stone circles was almost always looted, and a few human bones were scattered around the circles, I interpret these features as burials. Sector 3 is a series of plazas surrounded by cist tombs. Sector 4 appears to be a cemetery marred by looters' pits,

Figure 3.3. Suspension bridge connecting the town of Pay Pay to the archaeological site of Las Varas, Peru. (Courtesy of Howard Tsai)

though it lacks the circles of standing stones found in Sector 2. Such an unmarked, heavily looted cemetery is reminiscent of a burial ground from the coast.

Excavations were conducted in 2006 to test whether Las Varas was a highland colony like the vertical archipelago hypothesized by Murra. I utilized Stanish's methodology to determine whether the presence of Cajamarca-like pottery at Las Varas was due to colonization or, alternatively, trade. Four different scenarios could explain the presence of large quantities of highland or highland-influenced pottery and burial structures at Las Varas:

(1) Las Varas was inhabited by nonlocal people. (colonization)

(2) Las Varas was inhabited by local people who imported nonlocal artifacts or produced artifacts in imitation of nonlocal styles. (trade)

(3) Both local and nonlocal people occupied Las Varas. (coexistence)

(4) Nonlocal people replaced local people, or vice versa. (replacement, colonization)

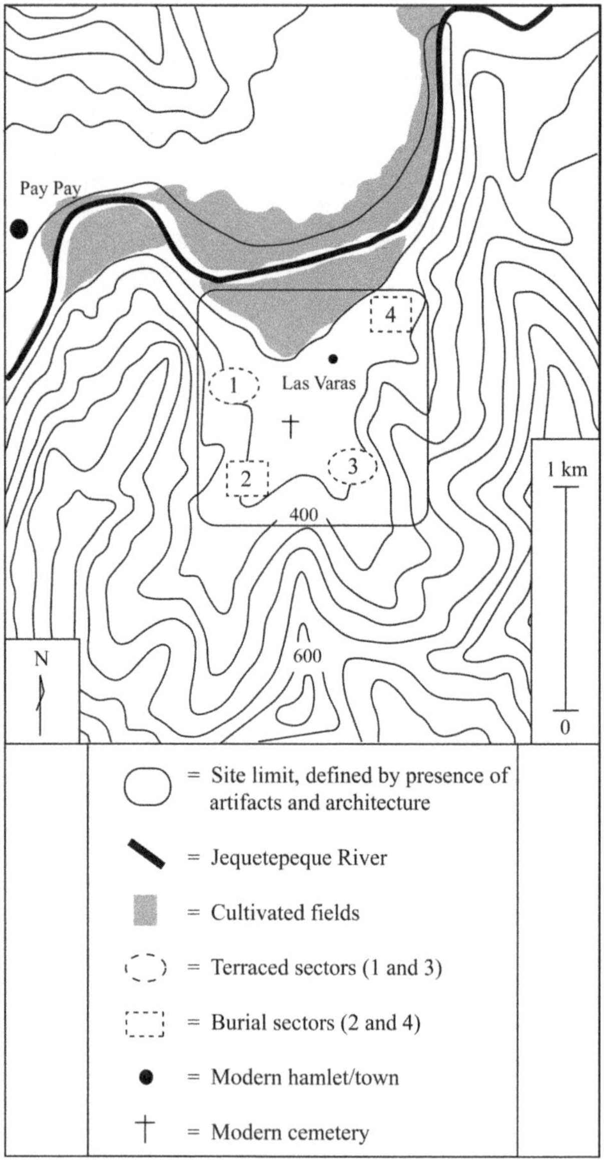

Figure 3.4. Map of Las Varas, showing various features and sectors within the site. Contour intervals at 50 m. (Courtesy of Howard Tsai)

By excavating the various sectors at Las Varas, I wanted to evaluate which scenario best explains the presence of Coastal Cajamarca pottery and highland cist tombs at the site. Results of the excavations confirmed some of the expectations for Scenarios 1 and 3 but also gave us some surprises. One unexpected finding was the use of ritual structures to differentiate two groups of visitors—highlanders versus coastal people (chapter 5). Radiocarbon dates revealed that Las Varas was occupied during the very beginning of the Late Intermediate (AD 1000), and therefore my data are better suited for understanding interactions in the pre-Chimu (Lambayeque) rather than the Chimu period. Even more crucial for our evaluation of Murra's fourth case is the overwhelming evidence, most of which came from excavations of the residential sector, demonstrating that the so-called Coastal Cajamarca style in fact originated from the chaupiyunga and not the coast (Tsai 2019). This revision of Jequetepeque culture history should make Andeanists abandon any easy coast/highland dichotomy and reconsider the chaupiyunga as an important agent in processes of ethnic interaction and exchange.

4

The Residences of Las Varas

Archaeologists working in the Andes have generally relied on artifacts and features from the domestic context as indicators of ethnicity and ethnic identity (Aldenderfer 1993; Stanish 1989). The assumption is that the household context, being a more "private sphere" or "internal domain" (Burmeister 2000:542), tends to conserve the practices and material culture of a particular ethnic group. One of Stanish's archaeological expectations of a colony is the presence of intrusive, foreign material culture, recovered in residential or domestic contexts, that contrasts with local traditions in the region. Las Varas's unusually high quantity of Coastal Cajamarca pottery, against the backdrop of a region dominated by coastal-style pottery, is suggestive of colonization, and therefore I decided to investigate the residential sector in an attempt to reveal the site's ethnic affiliation.

Data from our excavation of six residential structures at Las Varas are presented in this chapter. These residences, most of them located on hillside terraces, yielded evidence for domestic activities such as cooking, grinding, raising guinea pigs, and spinning (Figure 4.1). Our objectives in excavating the residential sector of Las Varas were to (1) document the range of household activities and (2) identify the style of household artifacts and architecture (e.g., pottery, spindle whorls, wall construction) that reflect the ethnic affiliation of the residents. Analysis revealed that the denizens of Las Varas adopted some highland material culture but preferred a unique chaupiyunga (so-called Coastal Cajamarca) style of bowls.

The Crystal House (Sector 1, Area B)

The Crystal House is located on a terrace in the residential sector (Sector 1, Area B) of Las Varas (Figure 4.1 and Figure 4.2). Since we found the highest concentration of quartz crystals here (totaling 785 g; see Tsai 2012a:Table 4.1), I named this structure the Crystal House. Our excavation of the Crystal House exposed 122 m^2 (Figure 4.3).

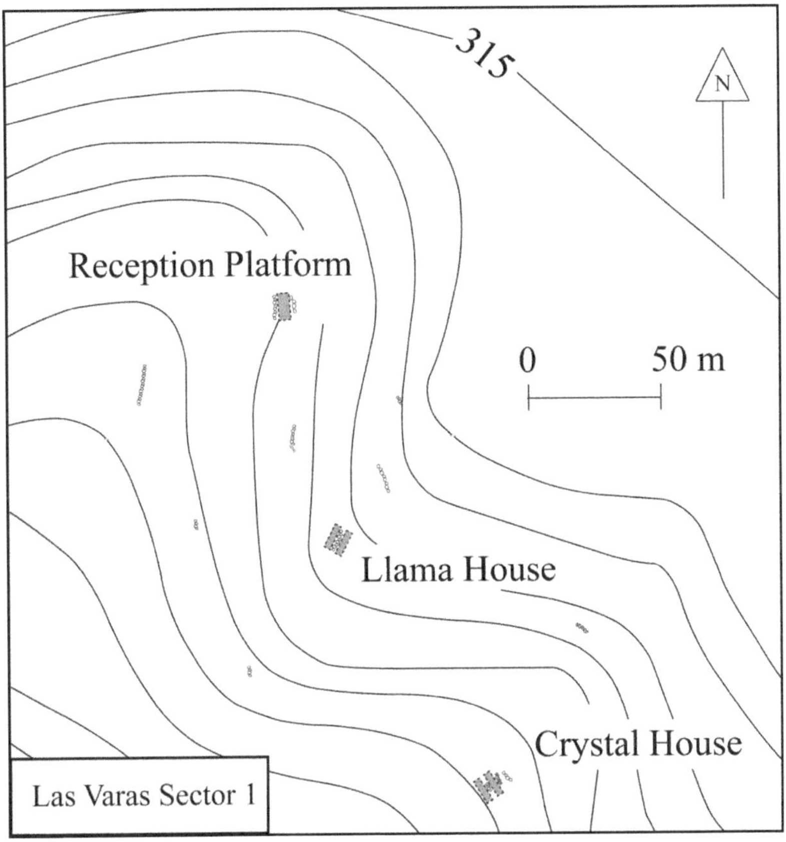

Figure 4.1. Map of Las Varas Sector 1. Gray boxes indicate excavated structures. Contour intervals at 5 m. (Courtesy of Howard Tsai)

The Crystal House was built atop a terrace formed by a retaining wall (Wall 1). The retaining wall was slightly curved to conform to the contours of the hill. The upper and lower levels of the terrace were connected by a corridor; a pillar-like stone jamb flanked the left side of the corridor's entrance on the lower level. The lower level likely served as a patio, and there we found small quantities of potsherds and a lithic core for producing chipped stones.

Visitors entering the patio from the south would go through a baffled entryway with low step and bench. North of this baffled entryway (inside the patio), beneath wall collapse, we found a broken ring-base bowl lying face down (Unit P4). The occupants of the Crystal House had apparently left this ring-base bowl when they abandoned this structure, and the wall later fell and crushed the bowl (Tsai 2012a:Figure 4.13).

Figure 4.2. Crystal House (Sector 1, Area B), Las Varas, looking northwest. (Courtesy of Howard Tsai)

Proceeding north, one reaches a corridor, 4.5 m long and 0.95 m wide, whose entrance is flanked by a stone jamb (Figure 4.4). A small piece of *Spondylus* shell was found inside the corridor, and a broken Lambayeque double-spout-and-bridge bottle had been placed in front of the stone jamb. The two spouts of this bottle were connected by a bridge made from twisted ropes of clay, and the bottle was decorated by two stylized animal heads attached to the body of the vessel below the spout (Tsai 2012a:Figure 4.14).

Walking up the corridor, one arrives at the upper level, which likely served as a kitchen equipped with a (1) guinea pig pen, (2) hearth, and (3) grinding slab (Figure 4.5). The guinea pig pen was a small stone circle (diameter 60 cm), and inside this circle we found guinea pig dung, pottery, crystals, and half of a metal tweezer. The hearth consisted of three stones placed close to the wall; a lens of ash was found in the middle of the three stones. We found orangish clay daub with cane impressions on the upper level (Units 9, 10, 13, 17, and 18), and a posthole (30 cm in diameter and 24 cm deep) in Unit 1, next to the guinea pig pen. The daub and posthole suggest that the house once had a roof made from cane and clay plaster, providing shade for those working in the kitchen.

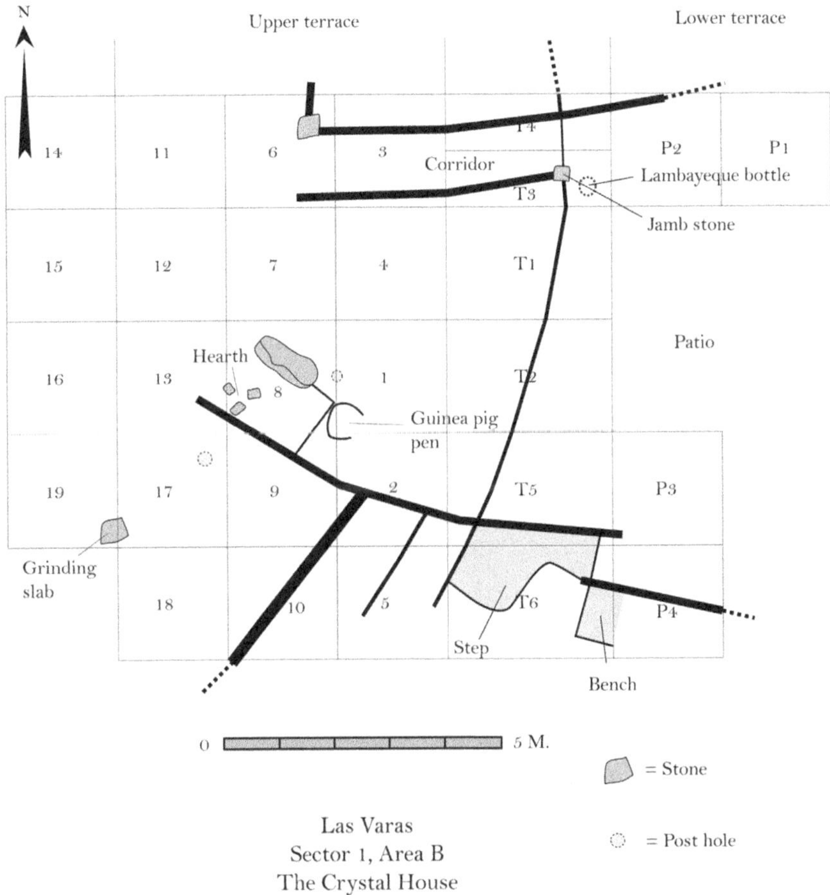

Figure 4.3. Plan of the Crystal House (Sector 1, Area B), Las Varas. Numbered squares represent 2 × 2 m excavation units. (Courtesy of Howard Tsai)

Trash served as fill for the building of terraces at the Crystal House, especially those in Units 5, 9, and 10. Materials recovered in the midden and construction fill of the Crystal House included pottery, spindle whorls, bones of camelids and cervids, land snails (*Scutalus* sp.), guinea pig dung, burnt maize cobs, chipped stone, and some small pieces of metal. Units 5, 9, and 10, which uncovered the middens and fill that made up the terraces, were some of our most productive units, turning up great quantities of pottery, animal bones, and chipped stone.

It is unclear when the Crystal House was abandoned. When the residents moved, they left the building as is without performing any kind of closing ceremony like the one conducted at the Llama House (see below). Rainfall in the

Figure 4.4. Corridor that connects the lower and upper levels of the Crystal House. Note stone jamb next to the entrance of the corridor. Scale, 1 m. (Courtesy of Howard Tsai)

middle valley, though not as heavy as in the highlands, can still be enough to erode soil and terraces on the hillside. Rain and wind would have weakened the walls, and wash from above would eventually give a final push and make them topple. Centuries later, as archaeologists excavate this structure, they would encounter a slope of dirt and collapse covering the remnants of the original walls below (Figure 4.6).

Crystals in the Ancient Andes

Quartz crystals, in the form of bars or chipped flakes, have been found in archaeological sites in the Andes, such as Pachamachay (Rick 1980:180), Huaricoto (Burger and Burger 1980), Pacopampa (Rosas and Shady 1970), Chavín (Burger 1998:201–203), Chinchawas (Lau 2010:301), and Chotuna (Donnan 2012:86–90). At Huaricoto, an offering of burnt crystals and shells was found in a hearth dating to the Late Preceramic, 2200–1800 BC (Burger and Burger 1980:28). At Las Varas, we did not find burnt offering of crystals, but we did find chipped crystals and crystal bars in the construction fill (such as those from the Crystal House) or in stratigraphic layers above the floor.

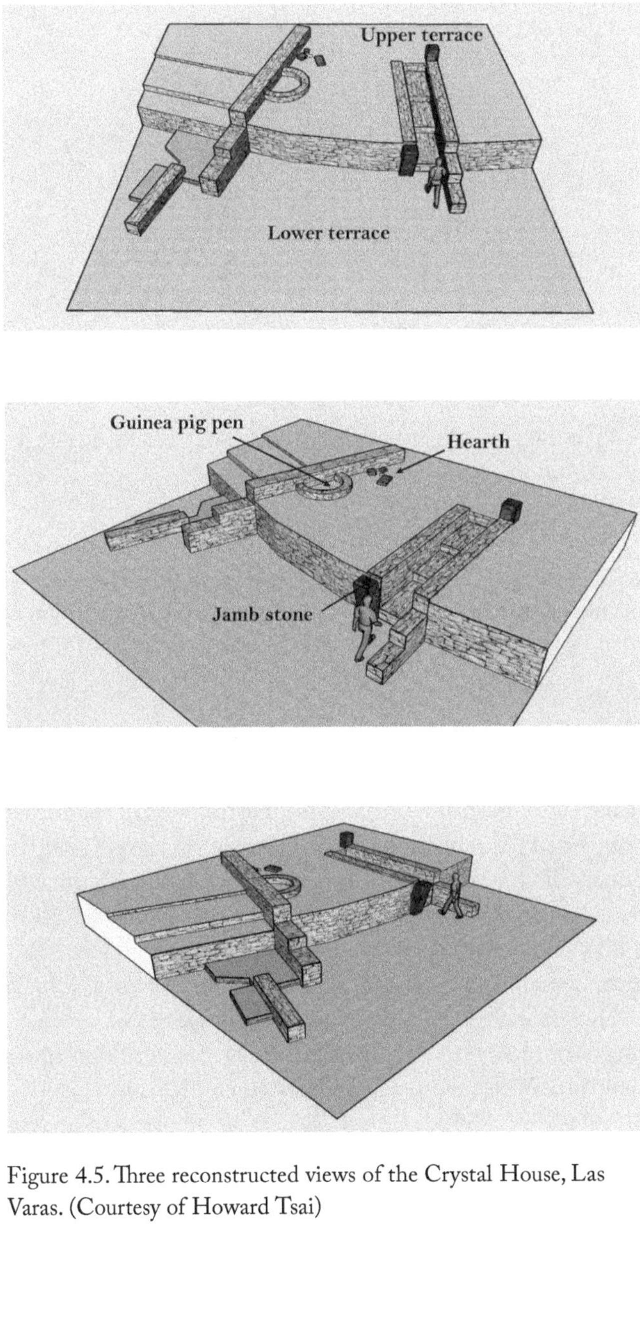

Figure 4.5. Three reconstructed views of the Crystal House, Las Varas. (Courtesy of Howard Tsai)

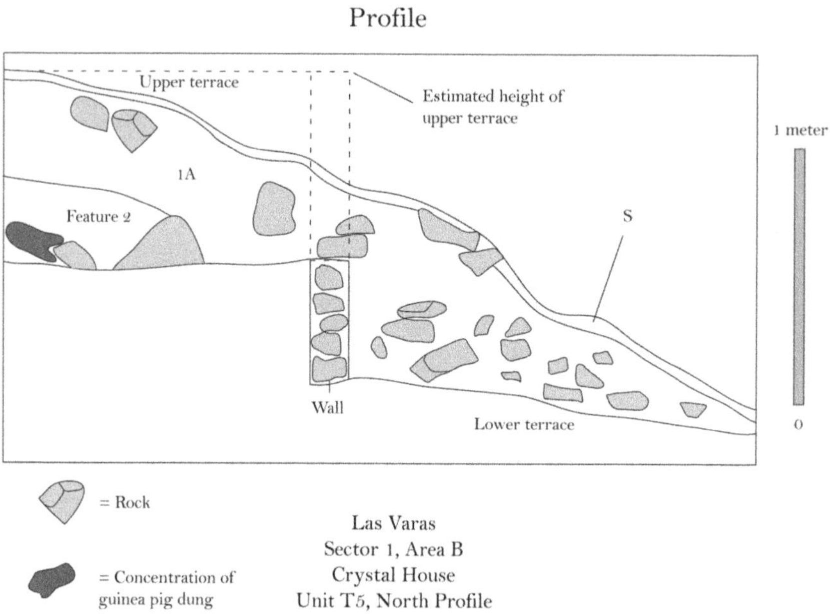

Figure 4.6. North profile of Unit T5 of the Crystal House: (S) surface, loose sandy loam (10YR 6/3); (1A) loose sandy loam with wall collapse (10YR 5/4); (Feature 2) loose sandy loam with guinea pig dung (7.5YR 5/4). (Courtesy of Howard Tsai)

Spanish documents refer to quartz crystals as "quispe" (González Holguín 1952 [1608]; Guaman Poma de Ayala 1993 [1615]) or "lacas" (Arriaga 1999 [1621]). Guaman Poma (1993 [1615]:249) illustrates a Quispiranpa, or a royal Inca litter decorated with shell and crystal. González Holguín (1952 [1608]:306) in his dictionary of Quechua defines "quespi" (or "quispe," a common surname in Peru) as crystal or anything transparent; "yurak quespi vmiña" (white quespi) referred to a diamond, "pucca quespi vmiña" (red quespi) to a ruby, "komer quespi vmiña" (green quespi) to an emerald, and "ancas quespi vmiña" (blue quespi) to turquoise. "Quespiñaui" (glass eye) came to mean glasses or someone wearing glasses (González Holguín 1952 [1608]:306). In modern Quechua, the word "qispi" means "glass" (Hornberger and Hornberger 2008:84).

Arriaga (1999 [1621]:34) describes "lacas" as small pieces of crystals used for personal charms or protective amulets ("conopa"). He notes that "in the lowlands, small pointed or angular crystals are regarded as conopas and are called lacas" (Arriaga 1968 [1621]:29). Quartz crystals are used by modern Peruvian shamans as part of their *mesa*, a cloth spread on the ground with carefully arranged ceremonial paraphernalia (Joralemon and Sharon 1993; Sharon 1978).

In the sixteenth century, Cristóbal de Albornoz (1989 [1580s]:186) made note of important huacas in the province of Cajamarca; three of the huacas from Cajamarca have either "quispi" in their names or are associated with crystal ("xriptal"):

> Angasquispi [blue crystal], huaca of the Caxas Indians, is a rock, which they say was clothed, next to the village of Biena.
>
> Quispi, principal huaca of these Cajamarca Indians of the ayllu Cuyosmango, was a rock where there is a source of water and crystal, in a hill next to the village of Sanchadas.
>
> [At] Utaran, huaca of the aforesaid from Cuyosmango, there are some rocks of crystal, which are in a hill called Utaran next to the town of Malcadan. [my translation]

The "ayllo Cuyosmango" likely refers to Guzmango, the modern town of the same name in the province of Contumazá, about 37 km southeast of Las Varas. The pueblo of "Malcadan" is probably San Lorenzo de Malcadan listed in a sixteenth-century census (Remy 1992:101), which later became Hacienda San Lorenzo (D. Julien 1993:Table 2; Pärssinen 2003:277–279) of Contumazá, 28 km southeast of Las Varas.

The Spondylus House (Sector 1, Area C)

The Spondylus House was built on two levels of terrace 97 m southwest of the Crystal House. Unlike the Crystal House, in which one terrace level was above the other, the terrace of the Spondylus House spiraled around a hill, with the lower level serving as a patio (2 × 4 m) to the east and an upper level, comprising a room (2 × 5 m), to the south. From the patio, one enters the room by going through a doorway flanked by a stone jamb (Figure 4.7). We excavated six units here, exposing a total of 24 m^2. Few artifacts (sherds, chipped stones, and crystals) were recovered in the Spondylus House, the only notable find being a piece of Spondylus near the inside corner of the room in Unit 6. No semicompact earth floor was found. Like the Crystal House, the Spondylus House featured a stone jamb entrance that opened to the east with a piece of Spondylus near the entrance.

Sector 1, Terrace 2

On the hills above the Reception Platform (chapter 5), we found some terraces that might have been part of a residence. Coastal-style ollas were present on the surface, so we placed a 2 × 2 m unit (Unit 1) to investigate this area. This unit was

Figure 4.7. Unit 6 of the Spondylus House, Las Varas, looking southeast. Scale, 1 m. (Courtesy of Howard Tsai)

Figure 4.8. View of the Llama House from the Reception Platform: (U) upper terrace; (M) middle terrace; (L) lower terrace. (Courtesy of Howard Tsai)

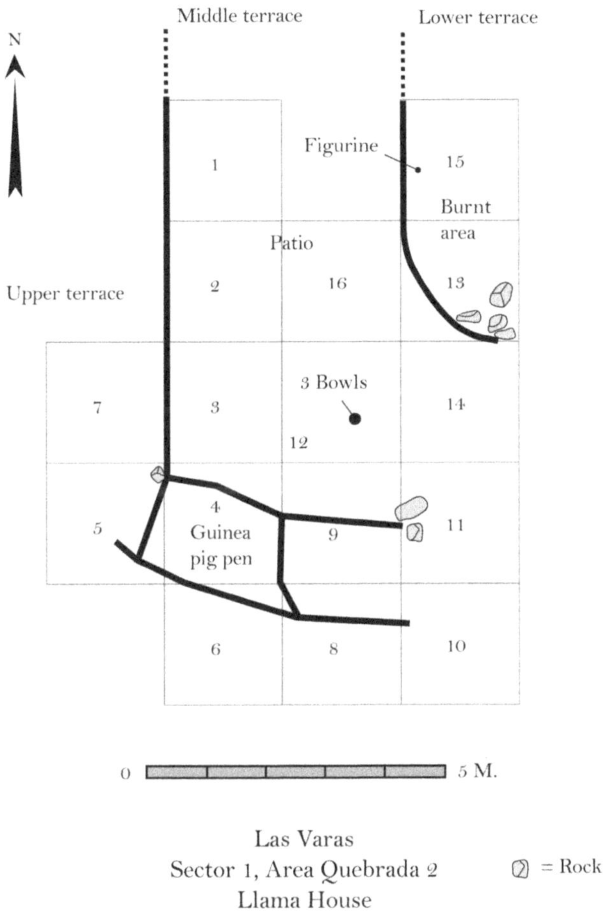

Figure 4.9. Plan of the Llama House. Numbered squares represent 2 × 2 m excavation units. (Courtesy of Howard Tsai)

not as productive as the others, and the cultural layers (Layers A and B), about 10–15 cm thick, were quite thin compared to those from the Crystal House or the Llama House. Artifacts recovered included potsherds, land snails, and bits of crystal. Such terraces, which lack architecture, are common at Las Varas; perhaps they supported ephemeral cane-and-daub structures that were not as elaborate as the stone constructions of the Crystal House or the Spondylus House.

The Llama House (Sector 1, Quebrada 2)

The Llama House is located in a ravine between the Crystal House and the Reception Platform (Figure 4.8). We exposed 64 m^2 of the Llama House, which extended over three levels of terrace (Figure 4.9). The lower terrace was covered

Figure 4.10. Middle terrace of the Llama House, showing an offering of three bowls in Unit 12, Level 1C. (Courtesy of Howard Tsai)

by a two-meter thick midden filled with pottery, guinea pig dung, ash, charcoal, animal bones, chipped stone, and other cultural materials. Burning had taken place on this terrace, darkening a large portion of the retaining wall. We found a semi-compact floor 2 m below the surface and a clay figurine 15 cm above this floor in a layer of ash (Layer E).

The middle terrace was a patio with a semi-compact floor. Like the lower terrace, it was overlain by thick layers of midden. The Llama House receives its name from the large number of camelid bones we found here, especially from Units 1 and 2. Some of the camelid bones show cut marks.

On the middle terrace, in Unit 12, we found three complete bowls whose style would be best described as Coastal Cajamarca (Figure 4.10); they were likely an offering to the house before it was ritually "sealed" and abandoned. In this sealing ritual, the entire patio was first covered by ash and charcoal (Layer D), the bowls were then set atop this layer of burnt material, and then the bowls were later covered by another layer of ash and midden (Layers C–B). The bowls were found in Layer C, a dark ashy layer filled with guinea pig dung and charcoal. Bowl 3 was set on its side, whereas Bowls 1 and 2 were stacked, face down. All

Figure 4.11. Las Varas Bowl 1 (diameter 15 cm, height 5.5–6.5 cm, ring base diameter 6.5 cm), found in Layer C, Unit 12, Llama House. Key characteristics are (1) painted interior design in red-on-white slip, (2) interior designs that consist of geometric and botanical motifs, (3) flaring rim, (4) white band painted on the exterior just below the rim, and (5) ring base. (Courtesy of Howard Tsai)

Figure 4.12. Las Varas Bowl 2 (diameter 17 cm, height 6 cm, ring base diameter 8.5 cm), found in Level 1C, Unit 12, Llama House. (Courtesy of Howard Tsai)

three bowls had ring bases and a band of white slip around the rim, typical of Coastal-Cajamarca-style bowls.

Bowl 1 has painted red-on-white interior designs consisting of concentric circles in the center and dot-and-crescents around the rim (Figure 4.11). The dot-and-crescents motif is frequently painted on the bowls of Las Varas and common on Cajamarca-style pottery of the highlands. The mid-valley (or Las Varas) version of this motif has only two crescents flanking the dot, whereas highland Cajamarca sherds often have multiple crescents.

Bowl 2 depicts two foxes, each facing a plant (Figure 4.12). Local residents

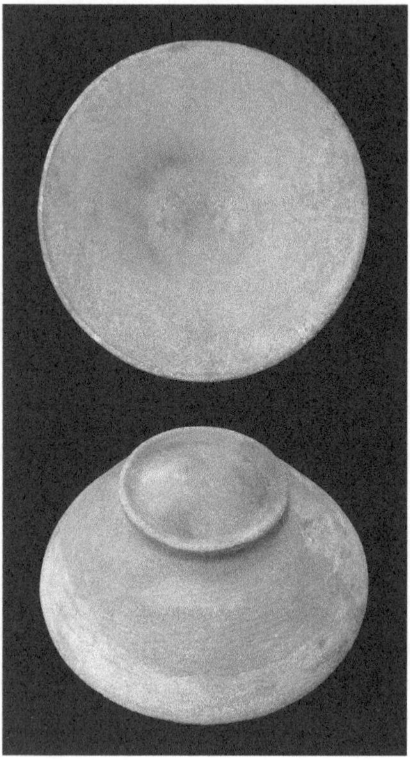

Figure 4.13. Las Varas Bowl 3 (diameter 15.5 cm, height 6 cm, ring base diameter 6.75 cm), found in Layer C, Unit 12, Llama House. (Courtesy of Howard Tsai)

tell me that the fruit of the sapote plant is a favorite among foxes. In the center is a postfiring incision drawn in the form of an arrow. This incision had been worn off at the bottom, indicating that the bowl had been *first* incised and then used. Repeated scrapes with a spoon, perhaps by someone hungry for that last scrap of stew, had eventually worn out the arrow.

Wooden spoons must have been the most common type of utensil in prehispanic Peru, but they are hard to find except in the driest of environments (see Owen 2005:Figure 13 for a set of wonderfully preserved wooden spoons from the Osmore drainage, southern Peru). We did not recover any wooden spoons at Las Varas, but we did find four fragments of ceramic spoons at the Llama House. Three fragments were tips that came from two different spoons; the fourth fragment was an almost complete spoon missing part of its tip. Ceramic spoons have been reported in the highlands of Cajamarca (Matsumoto and Ushino 1982: 188–189) but, as noted by Watanabe (2006:86), they are few in number compared to the amount of pottery one finds during excavation, suggesting that ceramic spoons were special objects produced and discarded infrequently.

Figure 4.14. Fragments of bowls found at Las Varas showing the volute (left, Sherd #8457 from the surface of the Llama House) and funnel (right, Sherd #2886 from Level 1D, Unit 2, Llama House) motifs. (Courtesy of Howard Tsai)

Bowl 3 has only a faint trace of its painted designs, which appear to have been worn off through extensive use (Figure 4.13). Close inspection shows that the painted motifs are the volute and funnel (Figure 4.14), a combination of elements commonly found on the bowls of Las Varas. The exterior surface was smoothed by repeated scraping, perhaps by a split cane like that found in the ceramic workshop at Maymi (Anders et al. 1998:241).

Beneath the three bowls was a layer of ash and charcoal (Layer D), and below Layer D was a semi-compact floor (Layer E) littered with crushed land snails. The floor was best preserved in Units 3, 12, and 16 and completely absent in Units 1 and 2. Once the floor had been exposed, we could see how the walls were constructed. Each wall was faced by the flat surfaces of angular, uncut stones. Larger stones were usually placed in the lower course upon which smaller stones were stacked and mud-mortared. It is unclear how the various terraces of the Llama House were connected, since we did not find corridors or steps that allowed access from one level to another.

No layers of ash and burning were found on the upper terrace. The most significant feature here was a large guinea pig pen, found in Unit 4, measuring 2 by 2 m. Besides being filled with guinea pig dung, this pen also contained five lithic cores used for producing chipped stone. Unlike the lower and middle terraces, no floor was found on the upper terrace. Outside and to the east of the

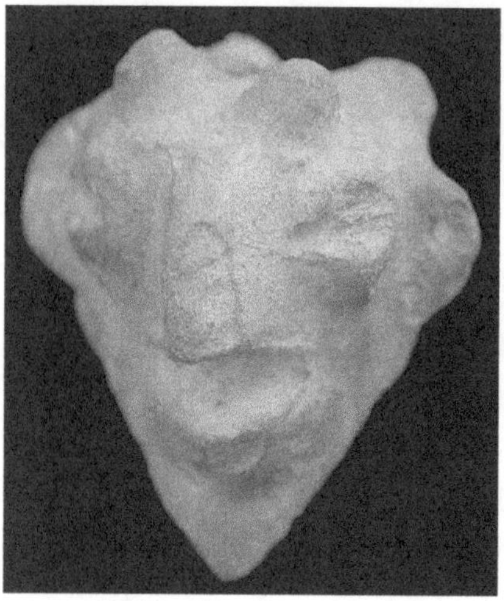

Figure 4.15. Modeled head of an individual (Las Varas Sherd #1119, height 3.8 cm) found in Layer A, Unit 3, Llama House. (Courtesy of Howard Tsai)

Figure 4.16. Modeled face of an individual (Las Varas Sherd #7128, height 5 cm) found in Layer E, Unit 15, Llama House. (Courtesy of Howard Tsai)

guinea pig pen (Unit 8, Layer A), we found what appeared to be the fragment of a panpipe with a modeled human face. Toohey (2009:Figure 7.19) reports similar panpipes with modeled human faces from Yanaorco, a Late Intermediate site near the city of Cajamarca.

Like the Crystal House, the Llama House had domestic refuse including pottery, spindle whorls, animal bones, land snails, guinea pig dung, and chipped stone. Unlike the Crystal House, however, heavy burning occurred at the Llama House and later it was deliberately covered by ash and burnt refuse.

Two fragments of pottery from the Llama House indicate that it was occupied sometime between the end of the Middle Horizon and the beginning of the Late Intermediate. The first piece is a modeled head of an individual wearing a four-cornered hat (Figure 4.15); the second is the face of an individual who has almond-shaped eyes and wears earspools (Figure 4.16). Menzel (1977) dates the first figure to Middle Horizon 2B, and Izumi Shimada (1990:315) dates the individual with the almond-shaped eyes to Early Sican (AD 700–900).

Two radiocarbon dates have been obtained from the Llama House: (1) a charred maize cob from Layer D of Unit 4 and (2) a charred maize cob from Layer C of Unit 12 (Table 4.1).

Table 4.1. Three Radiocarbon Dates from the Llama House and Reception Platform, Las Varas

Sample	Provenience	Material	Measured Age	13C/12C	Conventional Age	2 Sigma Calibration
Beta 287770, Las Varas #1231	Las Varas, Sector 1, Llama House, Unit 4, Layer D, 60 cm below surface.	Charred maize cob from guinea pig pen on the upper terrace.	810 +/– 40 BP	-11.5 o/oo	1030 +/– 40 BP	Cal AD 900 to 920, Cal AD 960 to 1040
Beta 287771, Las Varas #1344	Las Varas, Sector 1, Llama House, Unit 12, Layer C, 30 cm below surface, 40 cm above floor.	Charred maize cob from midden covering the patio (middle terrace), associated with offering of three complete bowls.	720 +/– 40 BP	-11.8 o/oo	940 +/– 40 BP	Cal AD 1020 to 1200
Beta 287769, Las Varas #811	Las Varas, Sector 1, Reception Platform, Excavation Unit 10, Layer F, 45 cm below surface, 30 cm below Floor 2, 20 cm above Floor 1.	Maize cob deposited after Phase 1 but before Phase 2, sealed between Floors 1 and 2 and Walls 1 and 3.	710 +/– 40 BP	-10.1 o/oo	950 +/– 40 BP	Cal AD 1010-1170

Note: Samples calibrated using IntCal04.

Figure 4.17. House 3C, Las Varas. (Courtesy of Howard Tsai)

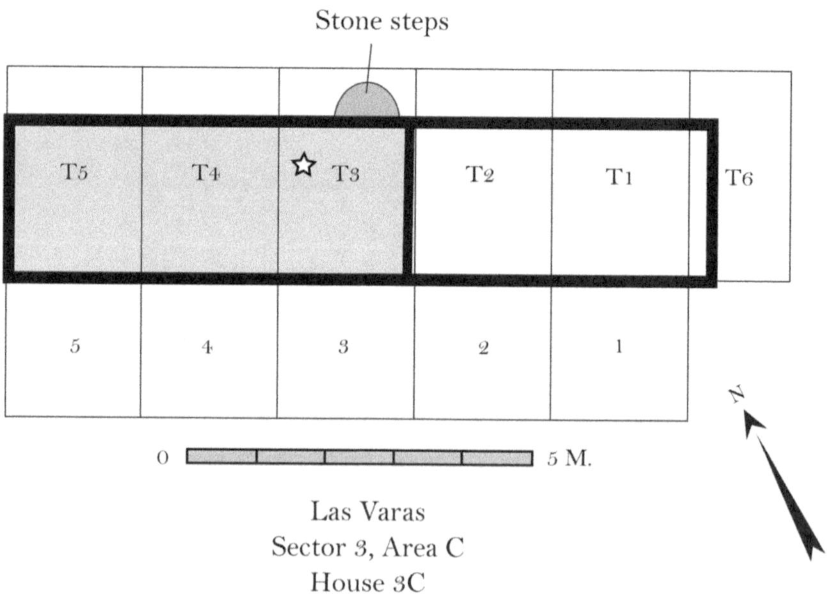

Figure 4.18. Plan of House 3C, Las Varas. Numbered squares represent 2 × 2 m excavation units. The gray area in Units T3–T5 indicates a floor 20 cm higher than the floor in Units T1 and T2. Star indicates where a mold was found beneath the floor. (Courtesy of Howard Tsai)

Figure 4.19. Fragment of panpipe (Las Varas #1850; length 4.7 cm) found in Layer B of Unit 1, House 3C, Las Varas. (Courtesy of Howard Tsai)

House 3C (Sector 3, Area C)

House 3C was not built on the hillside terraces of Sector 1 but on a flat area in Sector 3, 110 m north of the Plazas of the Malquis. Because House 3C was an isolated structure, at first I thought it was a storeroom. Measuring 10 m east-west and 2 m north-south, House 3C had stone steps on its north side leading up to the entrance (Figures 4.17 and 4.18). After finding large quantities of domestic refuse (ash, camelid bones, pottery, coprolites, and spindle whorls) along its south wall, I became convinced that this structure was a residence. The stone walls were likely the foundation for cane-and-daub fences, since there was not enough rubble around House 3C to suggest that the original stone walls reached more than a meter high.

We excavated outside House 3C along its south wall, starting at the eastern end (Units 1 and 2) where we found pottery, ash, charcoal, cuy dung, camelid bones, and spindle whorls. The occupants of House 3C apparently dumped their trash behind the house. This accumulation of trash petered out toward the west and disappeared in Unit 5. In Layer B of Unit 1, we found part of a panpipe depicting a face with coffee-bean eyes (Figure 4.19). Its form is similar to the panpipe found in the Llama House. In Layer A of Unit 2, about 7 cm below the surface, we found the head of a ceramic figurine depicting a person with braided hair or a braided headdress.

We opened five 2-by-3-m units (Units T1–T5) and one 1.5-by-3-m unit (Unit T6) to excavate the interior of House 3C. The area that would become the

Figure 4.20. House 1D, Las Varas. Excavations have exposed a bench and stone steps on the right. (Courtesy of Howard Tsai)

interior of the house (Units T1–T5) was leveled, forming a semi-compact surface (Layer F). Above this semi-compact surface a layer of guinea pig dung (Layer E) was spread, and upon this layer of guinea pig dung the walls of House 3C were built, including a wall (Wall 5 in Unit T3) in the middle of the house, bisecting the interior space into two halves.

The south wall of House 3C was made from stones bound with mud mortar, with smaller stones set upon larger ones. The north wall and Wall 5 (internal dividing wall), by contrast, appeared to have been loose rows of stones without mortar.

After building the stone walls, a semi-compact earth floor (Layer D) was laid down on both sides of Wall 5. Then a layer of fill (Layer C), consisting of loose earth, pottery, and guinea pig dung, was deposited west of Wall 5, and another floor (Layer B) was constructed above this fill. In the end, the floor west of Wall 5 was 20 cm higher than the floor to the east.

Two artifacts suggest that a potter had lived or left paraphernalia in House 3C. A ceramic mold for making an eye was found in Layer C (fill below the floor) in Unit T3. In addition, in Layer B (midden) of Unit 2, we found a round

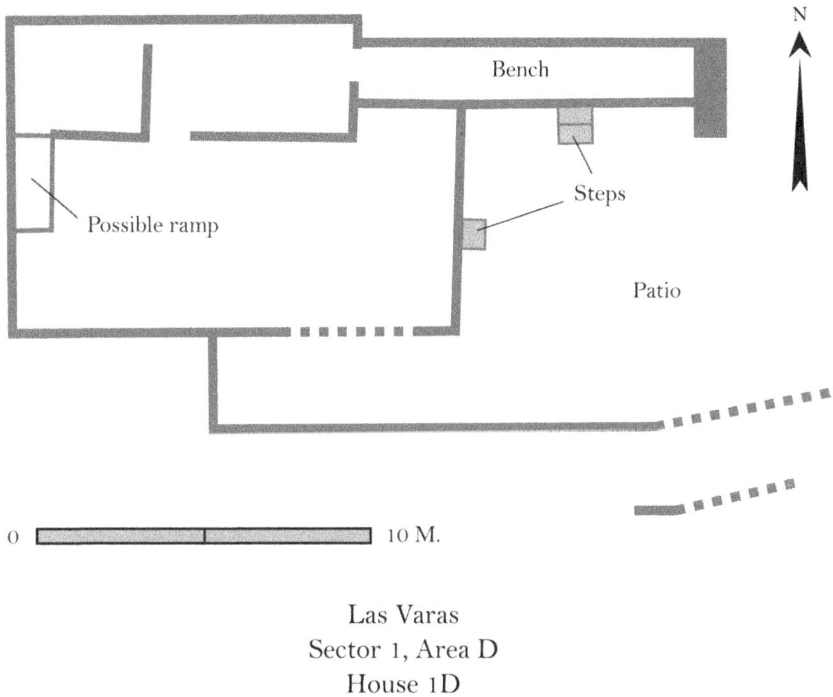

Figure 4.21. Plan of House 1D, Las Varas. (Courtesy of Howard Tsai)

piece of pottery, 12 cm in diameter, that could have served as a turntable for shaping pottery. Although these artifacts are not conclusive evidence, they suggest that pottery-making could have been one of the activities carried out at Las Varas.

House 1D (Sector 1, Area D)

House 1D is located in Sector 1, Area D, on the south side of a small hill 138 m east of the Spondylus House, overlooking the fields of Las Varas (Figures 4.20 and 4.21). Although House 1D has the most elaborate architecture at Las Varas, we were only able to excavate it during the last days of the project. If Las Varas were to be excavated in the future, more excavation units should be placed in the western portion of House 1D.

House 1D is typical of Las Varas residences in having a patio, terrace, and stone walls bound by mud mortar, but it is also unique and exceptionally elaborate for having an elevated bench/walkway accessible by stone steps that lead into a room on a terrace. Our excavations targeted this bench and stone steps located in the northeast corner of the house. The bench measured 2 × 10 m, and the stone steps measured 1 × 1 m; they were made from stones bound by orangish-brown mud mortar. We found cultural materials, including pottery, animal bones, and chipped stone. We did not find any compact earth floor. Another stone step, which we did not excavate, was found in the patio; it measured 1 m wide and 0.5 m long.

Even though we did not clear the rubble in the western half of House 1D, we could see an enclosure slightly higher than the adjacent patio and a possible ramp that connects the enclosure to a room built atop a higher terrace. In sum, House 1D was, architecturally speaking, the fanciest house at Las Varas; perhaps it was the residence of a high-ranking family.

Domestic Activities at Las Varas

Guinea pig pens were found in the Llama House and the Crystal House, indicating that the inhabitants were raising and consuming guinea pigs. Guinea pig dung was found in the construction fill and midden of all the residences except for the Spondylus House. Besides guinea pigs, we found remains of camelid (most likely llama), deer, shellfish, freshwater and saltwater crabs, and crayfish. Though we did not recover any fish bones, the finding of a small metal hook in the Crystal House (Unit 3) suggests that fishing had been part of the community's subsistence activities.

Heavy and light spindle whorls indicate that the residents were spinning camelid wool and cotton. We found awls or picks made from llama bones that resemble *wichuñas* or *pallanas*—picks for spacing the warp and the weft (Miller 1979:77–79). If these bone tools we found at Las Varas were indeed wichuñas, it would indicate that the residents were weaving textiles. Tourists visiting Chinchero (Cusco) today can still observe, and hear, the wichuñas in action. The sound of Chinchero women weaving, besides the intermittent chatter and laughter, is this constant buzz of slamming weaving swords and the staccato creaks, like those made from a rocking chair, of warps being picked.

We found 78 spindle whorls at Las Varas: 71 round discs (Figure 4.22) and 7 spheres. The disc whorls are generally heavier than the spherical ones, and this difference may relate to the thickness of the thread being spun. The heavier discs could have been used to spin coarse llama hair, and the lighter spheres to spin cotton (Vaughn 2009:121); this difference might explain why disc whorls are more commonly reported for the highlands and more spherical whorls are reported for the coast, where cotton is grown. Two weight classes of spindle whorls have also been documented for Mexico, where the heavy whorls were used for spinning maguey fiber and the light whorls for spinning cotton (M. Parsons 1972, 1975).

The disc whorls were made by grinding the edges of a sherd into a round

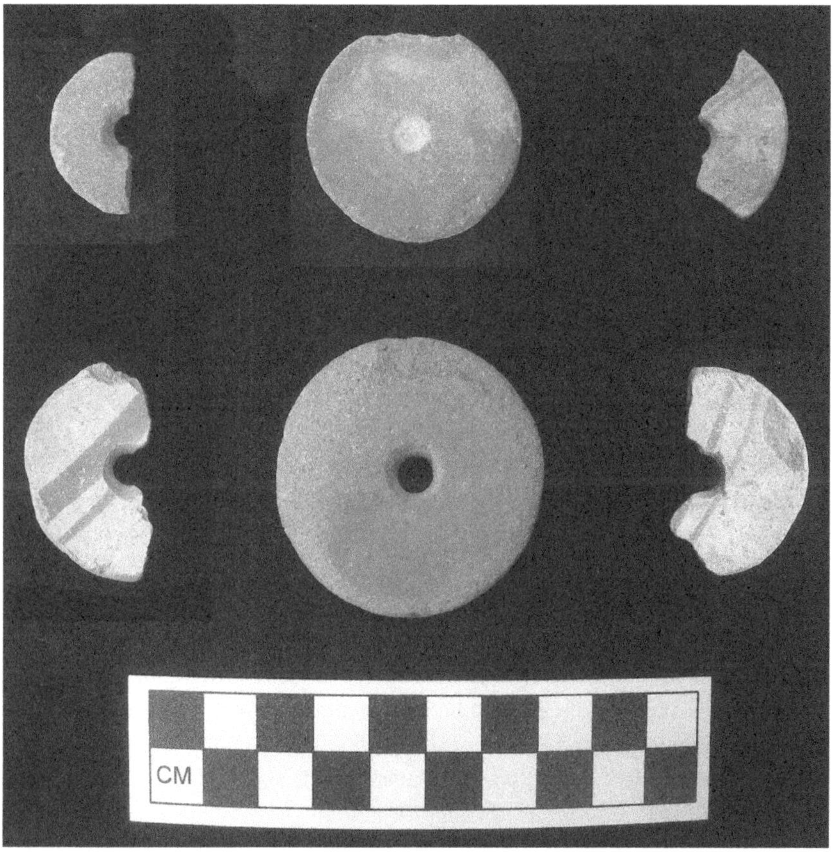

Figure 4.22. Disc-shaped spindle whorls, Las Varas. (Courtesy of Howard Tsai)

disc and then drilling both sides to create a hole in the center. Most of the discs found at Las Varas were unfinished: they range in shape from elliptical to round with incomplete perforations on one or both sides. None of the disc whorls were decorated, though some were made from the sherds of painted bowls.

Most of the spherical whorls from Las Varas were made from fired clay (n = 5), but we also found spheres made from stone and metal. Unlike the disc whorls, which were made from sherds, the spherical whorls were made by firing a small ball of clay incised with designs, and all but one of the spherical whorls from Las Varas were elaborately decorated. Ethnohistoric documents described specialists on the coast dedicated to the manufacture of spindle whorls (Hart 1983: 251). One spherical whorl depicted a miniature jar, and a stone spherical whorl was decorated with eight tiny inlays of blue-green gem.

The Anatomy of a Las Varas Painted Bowl

Excavation of the residences confirmed that, like what we had found on the surface, fragments of painted bowls from Las Varas were predominantly in the so-called Coastal Cajamarca style. The interior of these painted bowls has either red or black (but never both) geometric and zoomorphic motifs painted against a white background (see Figure 4.11) (Tsai 2019:124–127). A band of white slip wraps around the exterior of the bowl just below the rim. On some bowls this band is uniform in width, showing that the band has been carefully painted; on other bowls this band can be uneven or sloppy. Unlike painted vessels from the highlands of Cajamarca, whose exterior designs could be quite elaborate (with parallel lines and repetitive drawing of the dot-and-crescents motif), the Las Varas bowl has only this band of white slip as its exterior decoration. A ring of red or black slip is then painted on the very top of the rim. A sample of 1,116 painted bowl rims was recovered in our excavations, revealing an average diameter of 15 cm.

The upper portion of a Las Varas painted bowl, near the rim on the exterior surface, is often slightly thicker than the body. The presence of this slight protuberance leads Montenegro (1997:99) to suggest that the bowls were made by a "self-duplication" process: the potter takes a finished bowl, and, using it as a mold, pushes a clump of clay into it to form another bowl. The pressing would result in a pronounced thickening near the rim. I think Montenegro's hypothesis is very probable since I have observed many bowls at Las Varas with this kind of thickened rim.

The vast majority of the bowls are supported by a ring base averaging 7 cm in diameter (n = 552); a few bowls, usually the smaller ones with diameters less than 12 cm, have tripods. The ring bases are made separately from the body and are later attached before firing; close inspection of bowl fragments reveals a joint line between the ring base and the bottom of the bowl. Sometimes we find pieces of ring base that have fallen off a bowl.

A curious feature of Las Varas painted bowls is the occasional presence, in the interior surface, of postfire incisions. As Bowl 2 from the Llama House demonstrates, extensive usage occurs *after* the bowl was incised. We have documented a variety of postfire incisions (n = 28) at Las Varas, and the uniqueness of each incised symbol suggests that the incision may have been an owner's mark. It is important to distinguish postfire versus prefire incisions. The prefire mark allows the potter to distinguish his pot from other pots that have been piled together and fired within a single batch (Donnan 1971:465). The prefire mark identifies the potter or maker, whereas the postfire mark perhaps indicates the user or owner of that bowl, like the signature or "ex libris" sticker on a book's inside cover.

The shape of Las Varas bowls suggests that they were used for serving food or drinks. Tschopik (1950:208) recorded a type of bowl called *čuwa* in Chucuito, Peru, which may be a good analog for bowls from Las Varas:

> Bowls. The ordinary bowl, čuwa, is fairly standard in size, and has a diameter of 6 or 7 inches and a height of about 3 inches. Most bowls of this type have ring bases, and are slipped and painted with cursive designs in red or red and white. These vessels are used principally as food bowls, and are held to the lips by the base during meals, since spoons are not employed in eating. The čuwa is also filled with melted fat, supplied with a rag wick, and used as a lamp, on which occasions it is designated meča čuwa (from Spanish, mecha, "wick"). On other occasions, the bowls are employed as covers or lids for ollas and chicha jars, or are filled with glowing coals and used as incense burners. A second type of bowl, designated platilo or platil čuwa, has a flaring lip and lacks the ring base. These bowls always have painted decoration in red and white, and are employed as food bowls in weddings and on other festive occasions. Formerly, a generation ago, the bride and groom at a wedding jointly ate a special dish, timpu, from such a bowl in order to symbolize their union.

Complete bowls were very rare in our excavation—the vast majority of them had been found in fragments. Besides the three complete bowls found at the Llama House, we found a miniature tripod bowl that somehow managed not to break when it was discarded. At San José de Moro, complete Coastal Cajamarca bowls were found in burials as offerings. Hence the neatly placed, complete bowls at the Llamas House must have been ritually deposited and functioned as an offering for the structure's closing ceremony.

Origin of the "Coastal Cajamarca" Style

Resembling Cajamarca pottery but less complicated in their design, the painted bowls of Las Varas are abundant at the site, yet bowls of a similar style have also been reported on the coast. So where exactly did this unique style of painted bowls come from? Such Cajamarca-like bowls were first reported in the Jequetepeque Valley by Hans Disselhoff (1958) in his excavations of San José de Moro. Paul Kosok (1965:122), visiting Moro years later, made a limited surface collection and illustrated that same style of pottery in his book. Shimada (1982:173) also found Cajamarca-like pottery at the site of Sican, and because it was suspected that the pottery was produced on the coast rather than in the highlands, the style was given the name "Coastal Cajamarca."

Ongoing archaeological research in the Lower Jequetepeque Valley had documented a Late Moche (AD 600–800) origin of the Coastal Cajamarca style at sites like Huaca Colorada (Swenson et al. 2011:120, 123) and San José de Moro

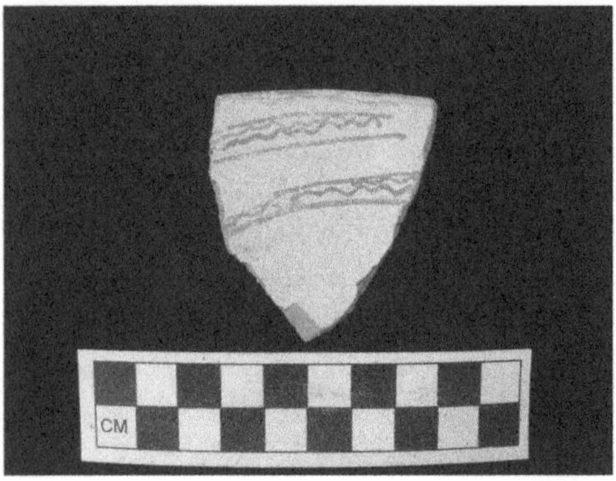

Figure 4.23. Examples of Coastal Cajamarca bowls with painted wavy line: *left*, rim fragment of painted bowl from Las Varas; *right*, top view of a Coastal Cajamarca bowl from San José de Moro painted with coiling wavy line (redrawn from Rubacado Yong and Castillo 2003:Figure 1.3d). (Courtesy of Howard Tsai)

(Bernuy and Bernal 2008). The earliest Coastal Cajamarca bowls, dating to Late Moche (AD 600–800) and Transitional (AD 800–900) periods, were painted with a wavy red line that spiraled out, like a coil, from the interior center (Bernuy and Bernal 2008:Cuadro 2), and white slip covered almost all of the exterior surface (Figure 4.23). After the wavy-line motif came the satellite and other red-on-white or black-on-white motifs, but later Coastal Cajamarca bowls had only a white band painted on the exterior, as described above.

The most detailed study of Coastal Cajamarca pottery to date is Jorge Montenegro's master's thesis (1997), in which he analyzed Coastal Cajamarca plates from the Lambayeque region and some Coastal Cajamarca sherds from the Jequetepeque and Zaña Valleys. He divided the Coastal Cajamarca style into two substyles: Sicán Painted Plates (Lambayeque) and Zaña-Jequetepeque (Montenegro 1997:4–5). D. Julien (1988:228) made a similar classification when he divided the Coastal Cajamarca style into three substyles, each with a different geographical origin. It appears, then, that the Coastal Cajamarca style varied from valley to valley. Montenegro's study concentrated mainly on the Lambayeque (northern) variety of the style, though he did include a small sample of the Zaña-Jequetepeque variant for analysis.

D. Julien (1988:229; 1993:262) and Montenegro (1993:144) both suggested that the Coastal Cajamarca style originated in the cis-Andean or chaupiyunga region rather than on the coast. Their hypothesis implies the existence of a mid-valley, chaupiyunga substyle within the broader Cajamarca tradition. Data from Las Varas have led me to agree with D. Julien and Montenegro: the vast majority of the bowls from Las Varas (more than 99%) is in the Coastal Cajamarca

Figure 4.24. Fragments of Coastal Cajamarca bowls from Las Varas painted with the "satellite" motif. (Courtesy of Howard Tsai)

style, and the sheer quantity and density (percentage within an excavation unit) of painted bowls from Las Varas are greater than those of any other reported site. In total, 37% (3,223 out of 8,785) of the diagnostic sherds found at Las Varas were pieces of Coastal Cajamarca bowls. In our excavations of residential middens, there were units (e.g., Units 13 and 15 of the Llama House) in which 40% of the diagnostic sherds were painted bowl fragments. These data constitute strong evidence that the Coastal Cajamarca style has its origins in the middle valley. Besides sheer quantity, other supporting evidence includes (1) diversity of designs, (2) presence in all contexts, and (3) association with a chaupiyunga-style domestic pottery.

A motif that frequently appears on the painted bowls of Las Varas is the "satellite," a design commonly found on the Coastal Cajamarca bowls of San José de Moro (Figure 4.24). But in addition to the satellite, we have documented

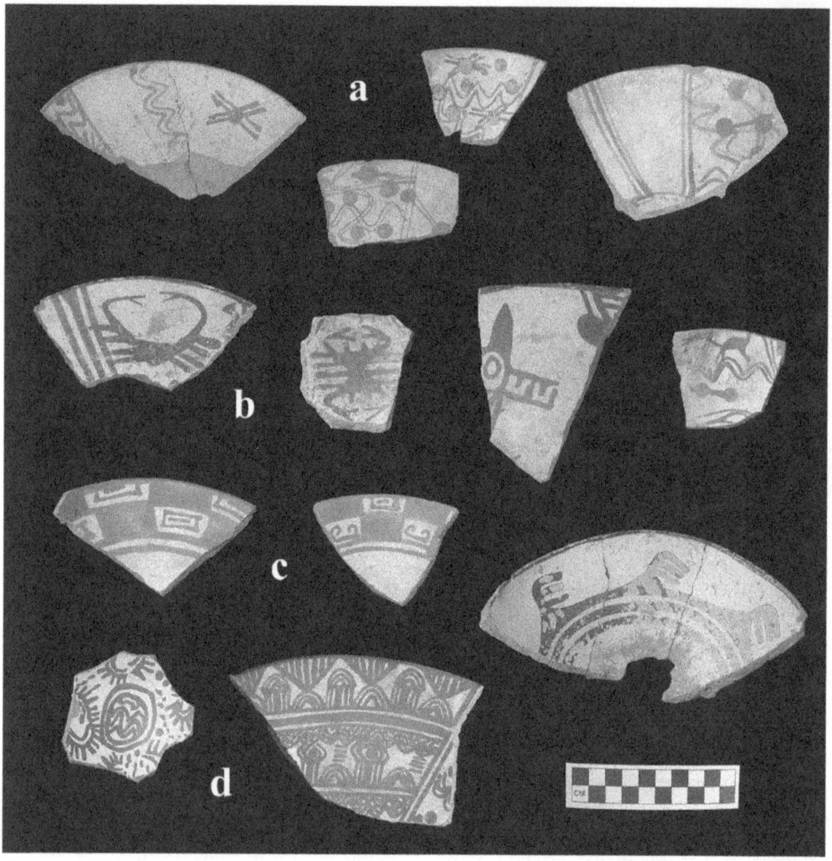

Figure 4.25. Fragments of painted bowls from Las Varas exhibiting a variety of motifs: (a) satellite; (b) animals including crab, fox, and llama; (c) checkerboard and wave; and (d) unique designs that appear only once. Scale 10 cm. (Courtesy of Howard Tsai)

a tremendous range of motifs on the bowls of Las Varas, including the volute and funnel (e.g., Llama House Bowl 3), animals such as llamas, crabs, and foxes (e.g., Llama House Bowl 2), and geometric designs such as the chessboard, fish-net, and concentric circle (Figure 4.25). This wide variety of painted, Cajamarca-influenced designs has not been reported from any site on the north coast. If we assume that the center of diversity is the center of origin, then the coast must have been the recipient, rather than the origin of this substyle of Cajamarca pottery. In other words, potters in the chaupiyunga had developed a diversity of painted designs of which only a limited set of motifs, such as the satellite, had been sent to the coast.

At Las Varas, the painted bowls were recovered in residential, public/ritual, and funerary contexts. In the residences they were found in the middens, construction fills, and floors. Away from the residences, fragments of these bowls were found scattered across the surfaces of public plazas and cemeteries. Their appearance in every context suggests that the painted bowls of Las Varas had been a normal, everyday object for the chaupiyunga people who produced, used, broke (accidentally or ritually), and finally discarded them. By contrast, archaeological excavations on the coast have reported the painted bowls only in burial or ritual settings. For someone living on the coast, then, the Coastal Cajamarca bowl represented an exotic, imported good from the chaupiyunga, to be used and placed solely in special and non-quotidian contexts.

Lastly, the Coastal Cajamarca style, out of all the ceramic traditions of ancient Peru, must have been the strangest for having just *one* form of vessel: bowls. Where was the rest of its family—pots, jars, tumblers, beakers, vases, and mugs? Our excavations at Las Varas uncovered a domestic ceramic assemblage alongside Coastal Cajamarca bowls: cooking and storage vessels made not in the coastal style but resembling those of the highlands (Figures 4.26 and 4.27). A prominent pottery form at Las Varas is similar to the highland type "Cajamarca Coarse Red" (Matsumoto 1982:107–108; Toohey 2011:188) characterized by jars with an everted rim, a red-slipped surface, and applique decoration. Viewed in profile, the everted rim flares outward in a curve or, alternatively, it can form a sharp, angular bend at the neck (Figures 4.26 and 4.27; compare with Matsumoto's [1982:107] Cajamarca Coarse Red Forms 4 and 5). The surface is painted with red slip and sometimes attached with appliques like meandering bands and cross-incised nubs, decorative elements typical of highland Cajamarca Coarse Red. The meandering band applique is made from a small coil of clay attached on the exterior surface to create a serpentine line; this line is then repeatedly incised to make multiple segments, like the sections of a worm (Figure 4.26c). The cross-incised nub is made from a ball of clay that is applied to the body of the vessel and then quadrisected to form an "x" (Figures 4.26b and 4.26e). Some rims are decorated with finger-impressed or incised designs (Figure 4.26a), and some jar handles are incised with multiple parallel lines running top-to-bottom (Figure 4.26d).

A large cauldron was supported by a ring base or tripod, which we found as detached fragments, indicating that they were first made separately and then attached to the bottom of the vessel (Figure 4.26g). The ring bases measure 10–15 cm in diameter. These kinds of annular and tripod support are commonly found in the northern highlands, including Cajamarca (Matsumoto 1982:Plate 38b) and Huamachuco (McCown 1945:Plate 23g). In addition, we had recovered pieces of ceramic spoons, a class of artifact associated with the material

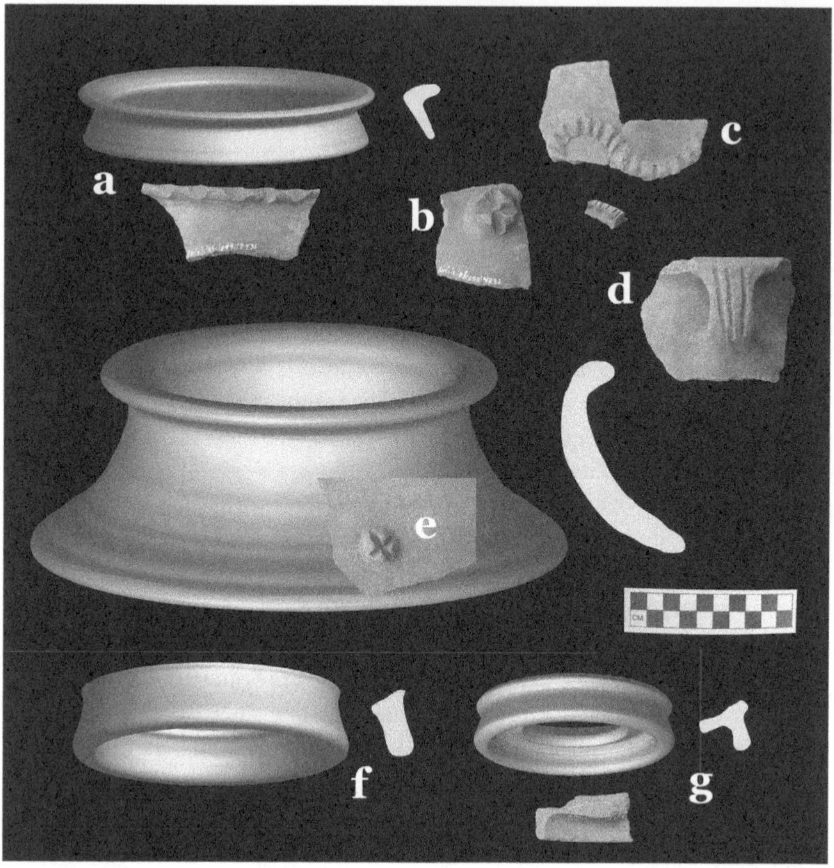

Figure 4.26. Las Varas pottery, not including painted bowls: (a) angular everted jar rim, diameter 17 cm, with finger-impressed decoration around the rim; (b) applique with cross incision; (c) serpentine applique; (d) jar handle incised with vertical lines; (e) everted jar rim, diameter 22 cm, with cross-incised applique; (f) rim base, diameter 15 cm; (g) rim base, diameter 11 cm. 3D reconstructions made using Adobe Illustrator "3D Revolve Effect." Scale 10 cm. (Courtesy of Howard Tsai)

culture of highland Cajamarca. One highland pottery form not found at Las Varas, however, is the "strainer" or "colander" form with multiple holes or perforations cut out of the vessel's body (Lau 2010; McCown 1945:Plate 22kk; Toohey 2011:180–181). Also absent from the Las Varas assemblage is the coastal "grater," characterized by multiple semilunar depressions incised in the ceramic vessel's interior surface (Donnan 1997:Figure 19e). In sum, the domestic or utili-

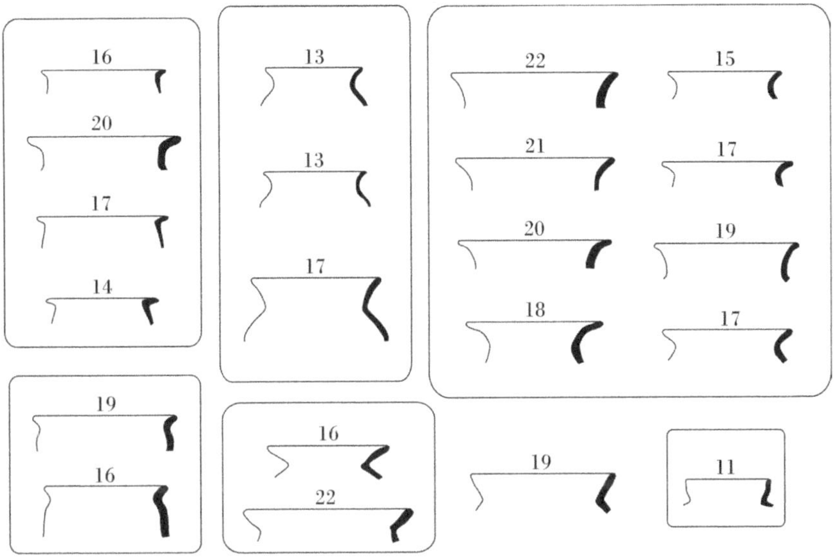

Figure 4.27. Rim profiles of pottery (pots and jars), Las Varas. Number indicates diameter of vessel in cm. Vessel on the lower right (diameter = 11 cm) is a coastal-style carinated *olla* found at Las Varas. (Courtesy of Howard Tsai)

tarian pottery from Las Varas is quite different from that of the coast; it is more reminiscent of highland traditions, consisting of jars with everted or angular rims, applique decoration of the body, and tripod or rim base support.

The pottery assemblage of Las Varas, taken together, forms a complete set of vessels that would qualify as a true archaeological culture. Given this evidence, the case for a coastal origin of "Coastal Cajamarca" has become very unlikely. The "coastal origin" hypothesis would imply that people in the chaupiyunga (Las Varas) used highland-like domestic pottery with appliques and everted rims but imported almost all of their bowls from the coast, made by coastal potters who themselves were imitating a highland style. A convoluted scenario indeed.

If the Coastal Cajamarca style did not come from the coast, then a better label must be warranted—perhaps "chaupiyunga" or "mid-valley" Cajamarca? The Wari style had similarly been called "Coastal Tiahuanaco" (Goldstein 2005: 88–90 gives a thorough background on this terminology), and the history of this misnomer should serve to remind us that the place of initial discovery does not necessarily point to the place of origin. In regard to ceramic typology, I would prefer a label that avoids conflating culture, political unit, ethnicity, and time period. The type-variety system is less misleading than typologies with strong cultural connotations (like Moche, Chimu, Chavin), but even the type-variety typology, with its seemingly culture-neutral emphasis on paste and surface treatment, has its critics (Smith 1979).

I propose that "Las Varas Painted Bowl" is a useful category since, as described in the previous section, this type of pottery is a coherently packaged suite of form and design. By "coherently packaged" I mean that certain stylistic elements always co-occur, such as red- or black-on-white painted interior designs, painted white band wrapping the rim on the outside, a ring base, and the occasional postfire incision. Furthermore, these painted designs appear on only one class of vessel: bowls. Their center of distribution lies in the chaupiyunga zone of the Jequetepeque and Zaña Valleys, appearing around AD 900 and phasing out by perhaps AD 1300. A tentative chronology of chaupiyunga painted bowls is outlined in chapter 6. In sum, data from Las Varas have confirmed D. Julien's and Montenegro's hypothesis that the Coastal Cajamarca style originated from the chaupiyunga (Tsai 2019). By pinpointing the origin of this style in the middle valley, many puzzling aspects of these painted bowls are now resolved.

Las Varas: What Was It "Ethnically"?

Returning to my initial question—was Las Varas a *highland* colony?—the answer must be "no," because material culture from the site's domestic contexts appears to be local, that is, chaupiyunga, rather than transplanted from the highlands. If Las Varas were a colony at all, it must have been a chaupiyunga settlement established near the coast, perhaps as part of a gradual push by mid-valley populations toward the lower valley. The Las Varas type of painted bowls (Coastal Cajamarca) resembles those from Cajamarca but ultimately constitutes a class of its own: a local, chaupiyunga variant.

Other lines of evidence, such as domestic architecture, spindle whorls, cooking pots, and storage jars, point to affinities with highland cultures. Like the domestic pottery of highland Cajamarca, the pots and jars of Las Varas were made with everted rims and decorated with appliques. The Crystal House and the Spondylus House, having stone jambs next to their entrances, were architecturally similar to highland buildings. Interestingly, both houses had a fingernail-sized *Spondylus* fragment placed on the ground near the stone jamb. Most of the spindle whorls at Las Varas were made from round ceramic discs, a type of whorl ubiquitous in the highlands. The appearance of highland cultural elements in the chaupiyunga zone had been reported in various Peruvian valleys, including the Chillón, Nepeña, Santa, Virú, and Moche. Despite this influence from the highlands, chaupiyunga communities, at least those in the Jequetepeque, had developed a unique material culture with a local flavor different enough to distinguish them from their *serrano* neighbors.

Its resemblance to highland pottery notwithstanding, what is absolutely clear is that the ceramic style of Las Varas is very different from that of the coast. Designs on Las Varas bowls were painted rather than press-molded; cooking pots and storage jars had everted rather than carinated or cambered rims; the surface of these pots and jars was decorated with applique rather than paddle-stamped. Though coastal-style sherds were present at Las Varas, they constituted a mere 5% of the assemblage (400 coastal-style sherds out of 8,681 total diagnostic sherds). To be discussed in the next chapter, most of the coastal-style pottery was found in a particular sector of the site: the Reception Platform.

Our excavation of the domestic contexts has been very productive and helpful for testing hypotheses regarding ethnic affiliation and population movement. Yet I am still not quite satisfied with the household approach to ethnicity. This reliance on household artifacts posits an ethnic "inner core" within the residence, as if only within the threshold of the house lies that family's true identity. This assumption is under-theorized and lacks "a concurrent examination of the process through which housing might be chosen as a symbolic communication of difference" (Stovel 2013:8). In the case of Las Varas, why did its residents choose to use and maintain a chaupiyunga style of pottery different from that of the coast? Why was there no mixing of styles? Why such strict maintenance of stylistic boundaries? These questions cannot be answered by assuming the naturalness of ethnic affiliation as revealed by household artifacts, lest we regress to the culture-as-nation paradigm described in chapter 1.

A more productive approach, I believe, resides in a framework that combines multiple contexts or settings to examine the intersection between the domestic/household/private sphere and the communal/regional/public arena. Identity in the private place takes on a different life in the public domain. In difficult political or diplomatic situations, strategic identities and categories are brought to the negotiating table. Surely they are not the same as those in the household, nor are they any less important. We should therefore not insist that a certain context (e.g., ritual, funerary, domestic) is more important than another; we should instead recognize that all sorts of identities, be they ethnic, economic, political, gender, and so on, are present at all times but manifest differently, depending on the context. It is the combination of data from both domestic and public contexts that will allow archaeologists to document the construction of ethnic identities. To illustrate this multicontextual approach, data from the ritual sectors of Las Varas will be presented in the next chapter to demonstrate the "digitization" effects of ritual in hardening social and ethnic boundaries.

5

The Ritual Boundaries of Las Varas

Ritual, according to Rappaport, conveys a kind of information that is qualitatively different from non-ritual communication. Not only is ritual message imbued with greater sanctity and truthfulness, but the consequence of ritual is the creation and reinforcement of social categories like those of age, gender, and ethnicity. Archaeologists treating ritual as mere supplication of supernatural beings need to consider this important aspect of ritual action.

Two ritual areas were excavated at Las Varas: the Reception Platform, located next to the western entrance of the site, and the Plazas of the Malquis, located near the southern entrance. By building these ritual structures near the edges of their community, the residents of Las Varas had effectively drawn a ritual boundary around their village, creating ethnic differences between people arriving from the coast and those from the highlands. These findings represent a unique and important case study on how archaeological excavation, unaided by historical documents, can uncover the process by which a community constructed its ethnic identity.

The Reception Platform

During a survey in 2005, I arrived at Las Varas for the first time after scaling a hillside ridge that overlooked the Jequetepeque River, the Gallito Ciego Dam, and a patch of rice field on the south bank of the river. On this ridge, we found fragments of painted bowls and traces of stone walls visible just above the surface (Figure 5.1). A year later (2006), we excavated this ridge and discovered one of the site's most interesting and enigmatic structures: the Reception Platform. During fieldwork, this ridge was designated Area A of Sector 1. Here, we found benches, plastered floors, and many coastal-style pottery such as paddle-stamped and cambered-rim ollas. The total area exposed at the Reception Platform was 74 m^2 (Figure 5.2).

Excavations revealed that visitors coming from the coast entered Las Varas via the Reception Platform, just as I did when I first arrived at the site; they then left behind some of their coastal-style pottery and marine shellfish. The struc-

Figure 5.1. Reception Platform at Las Varas, looking east. Excavations have exposed the T-shaped structure from the third and final construction phase of the platform. (Courtesy of Howard Tsai)

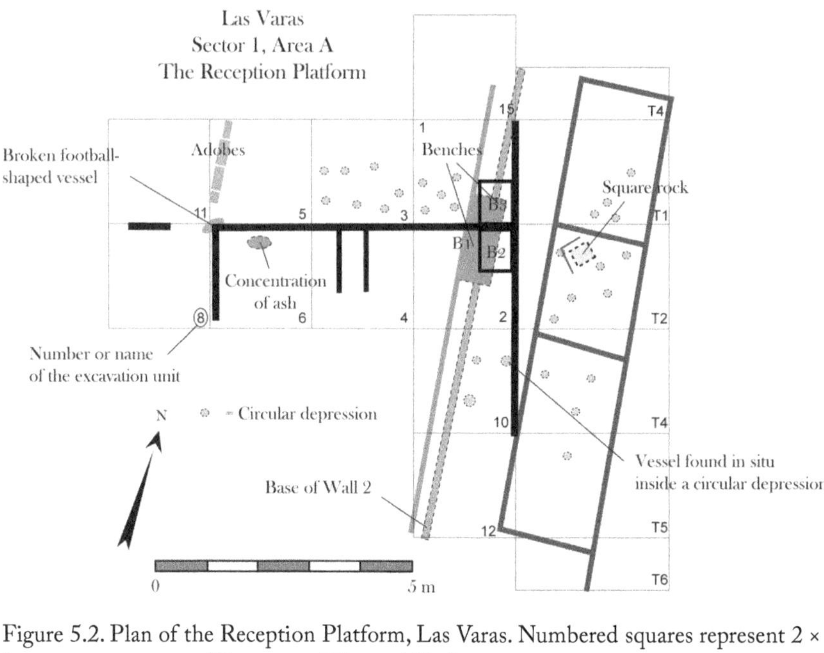

Figure 5.2. Plan of the Reception Platform, Las Varas. Numbered squares represent 2 × 2 m excavation units. (Courtesy of Howard Tsai)

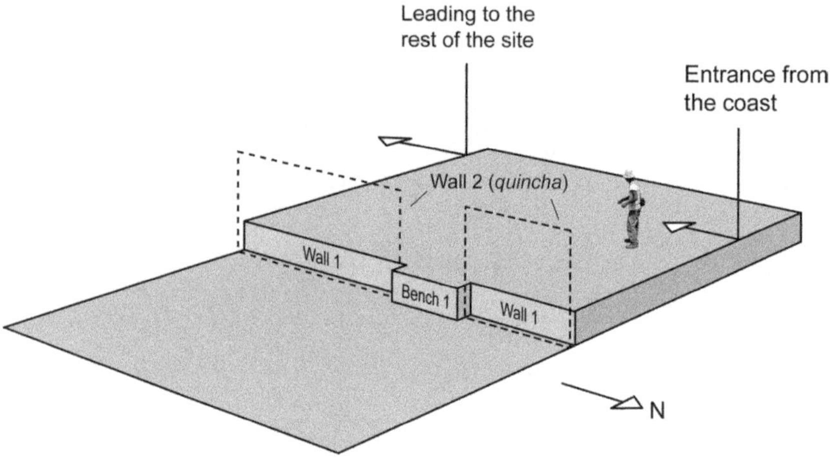

Figure 5.3. Reconstruction of Reception Platform during Construction Phase 1. (Courtesy of Howard Tsai)

ture, however, served as more than a tourist's signpost. In the following sections, evidence is presented to demonstrate the ritual function of the Reception Platform.

Architecture

In laying out the various building phases of the Reception Platform, my description proceeds from the earliest stage to the last. Since the earliest phase of construction was deeply buried and discovered last, the following sequence of reconstruction unravels like a backward reel of our actual experience in the field.

Construction Phase 1. During the first construction phase of the Reception Platform, a retaining wall (Wall 1) was built on the ridge's slope to create a terrace approximately 6 m long and 9 m wide (Figure 5.2). A rectangular structure, Bench 1, projected out from the middle of Wall 1; this bench measured 170 cm long, 40 cm thick, and 60 cm high. Bench 1 and the floors of the terrace were then plastered with daub. The fine quality of the floor (Floor 1) distinguished the Reception Platform from the residences: no plastered floors were found at the Crystal House, and the Llama House had only patches of poorly preserved floors. By contrast, the sturdy and compact floors of the Reception Platform were easily exposed by gently troweling and brushing away the overlying soil.

Two *quincha* (cane-and-daub) walls fanned out from the sides of Bench 1 (Figure 5.3). We did not find the actual remains of these quincha walls (Walls 2N and 2S); what we did find were lines of missing floor that would have been

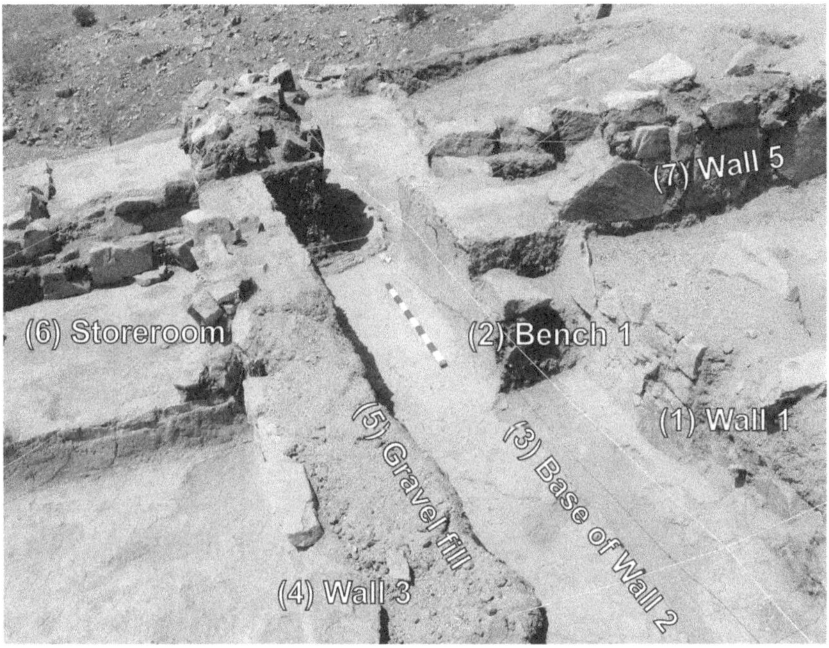

Figure 5.4. Reception Platform during Construction Phase 1 (looking south). Numbers in parentheses indicate the sequence of construction. Scale, 1 m. (Courtesy of Howard Tsai)

where the walls—made from stalks of cane—had been inserted (Figure 5.4). Fragments of cane-impressed daub were found along these lines of broken floor and against the sides of Bench 1, and from these clues I inferred the presence of two cane-and-daub walls projecting from Bench 1.

For someone standing on the Reception Platform during Phase 1, the quincha walls would have blocked the view of the valley except for a 1.7-m-wide gap created by Bench 1 (see Figure 5.3). Given the alignment of Bench 1 on a north-south axis (magnetic 2°/182°; see Figure 5.2), I suspect that this gap would have been used to observe the sunrise during the equinoxes in March and September.

At the end of Construction Phase 1, the quincha walls were removed. Wall 3 was built in front of Wall 1, and the space between them was filled with gravel chips obtained from the granodiorite bedrock to bury Bench 1. The top of this fill was then sealed with a clay floor (Floor 2). The use of clean fill was unusual since most construction fills, for example those from the residences, were full of garbage like potsherds, animal bones, and ash. By contrast, the Reception Platform's clean gravel fill had only a few pieces of pottery and a burnt maize cob.

Figure 5.5. Three storerooms built in front of Wall 3 (Construction Phase 2, Reception Platform, Las Varas). (Courtesy of Howard Tsai)

Radiocarbon dating of that maize cob placed the terminus post quem of Phase 1 to ca. AD 1090, around the time of Llama House's abandonment (see Table 4.1).

Construction Phase 2. During the second phase of construction, three small rectangular rooms, each measuring 3 × 2 m with walls 30 cm high, were built in front of Wall 3 (Figure 5.5). Circular depressions, 10–30 cm in diameter, were present on the floor of these rooms. Mud plaster lined the edges of some of these depressions, indicating that they were pot rests designed to hold the bottom half of a ceramic vessel (similar examples have been found in the US Southwest; see Adams 1983:Table 1), and not postholes. Indeed, in a pot rest in Unit 10 we found the bottom half of an olla whose surface was decorated with press-molded designs in the typical coastal style. The presence of pot rests means that the rooms served as storage units during Phase 2.

A row of four adobes was found 10 cm below the surface of Unit 5. It ran parallel to Walls 1, 2, and 3, and therefore probably dates to Phases 1 or 2, or both. The adobes were not standardized in size—their lengths varied between 21 cm and 50 cm, their widths varied between 15 cm and 22 cm, and their average thickness was 10 cm. These were the only adobes found at Las Varas.

Figure 5.6. Square rock found in the Reception Platform, Las Varas. North arrow, 20 cm. (Courtesy of Howard Tsai)

At the end of Phase 2, the storerooms were filled with earth that included some sherds and animal bones. Above this fill was a hard compact layer, and sitting atop this hard layer was a flat square rock measuring 30 × 30 × 15 cm (Figure 5.6). This square rock was flanked by two miniature earthen walls measuring just 20 cm high and 5 cm thick. The rock was then covered with earth, and afterward no structure was built above this square dedicatory stone.

Construction Phase 3. In the third and final construction phase of the Reception Platform, two walls (Walls 4 and 5) forming a T were built on the upper level (Figure 5.1). Two small square structures (Benches 2 and 3), each measuring 80 × 80 × 30 cm, were built at the intersection of Walls 4 and 5. Bench 3, located north of Wall 5, was mostly destroyed, whereas Bench 2 was undamaged (Figure 5.7). Walls 4 and 5 have a slightly different orientation from earlier walls, with Wall 5 pointing approximately 11 degrees north of true east (magnetic 81°).

Two parallel lines of stones slightly longer than a meter were built against the south side of Wall 5. Guinea pig pellets were found between these two walls, suggesting that they might have been used as a small pen. A concentration of ash, 30 cm in diameter, was found at the southwest corner of Wall 5. The area

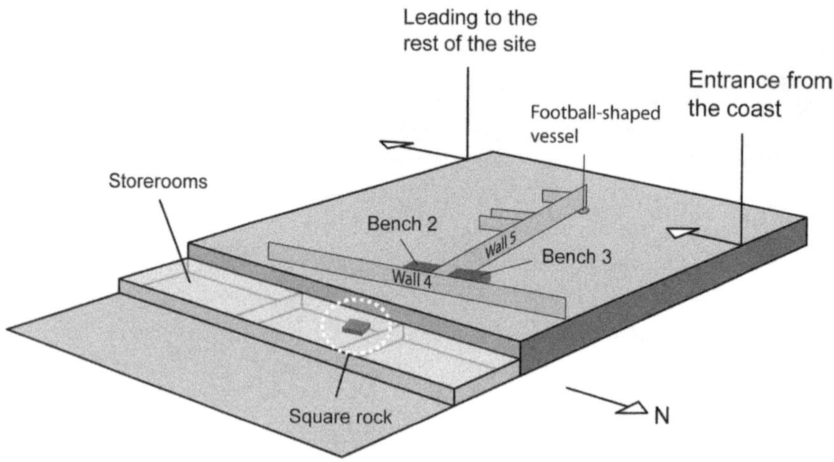

Figure 5.7. T-shaped structure from Construction Phase 3, Reception Platform, Las Varas. Note two small, bin-like benches at the corners of the T-junction. Scale, 1 m. (Courtesy of Howard Tsai)

north of Wall 5, by contrast, appeared to be "empty" since we did not find any stone structures or signs of activity. Finally, an American football–shaped vessel was found below Wall 5 near its western end (Tsai 2012a:5.24).

Evidence of Ritual at the Reception Platform

The Reception Platform was unique in having storerooms, pot rests, adobes, and other features not found elsewhere at the site. I interpret the platform as a ritual structure because it contained what Renfrew and Bahn (1996:391) called "attention-focusing devices" or "special fixtures." For example, Benches 2 and 3 were built directly above Bench 1, even though they were oriented to different directions (see Figure 5.2). By placing a square rock above the center of the storerooms, attention was focused on the central part of the structure. The exact ritual meaning of these elements, however, is unclear.

Other lines of evidence besides architecture distinguish the Reception Platform from the residences. A human phalanx was found in the fill of the central storeroom (Unit T2), which dates to the end of Phase 2. At Las Varas, this phalanx is the only human bone not found in a burial or cemetery; no human bones were found in the residences. I have sorted through all the human osteological and nonhuman faunal materials from Las Varas, and this fingerbone from the Reception Platform is the only human remain found in a non-burial context at the site.

The Reception Platform also has the largest quantity of the marine gastropod *Polinices uber* at Las Varas. The amount of *Polinices* (n = 193) found at the Reception Platform contrasts sharply with its scarcity in the residential areas (n = 6). It appears that when coastal visitors brought shellfish to Las Varas, *Polinices* were somehow left at the entrance of the site, whereas other species were consumed in the residential areas. Marine shells were found in almost all sectors of Las Varas, but it was just this particular species, *Polinices*, that was found in highest proportions at the Reception Platform (Tsai 2012a:212).

The Reception Platform has more coastal-style pottery than the residences do—81% of all the coastal-style sherds found at Las Varas were concentrated at the Reception Platform (see Table 5.1). This is not a result of sample size bias, that is, more sherds being found at the Reception Platform. In terms of total number of ceramic fragments found, the Llama House takes the lead in yielding 5,098 pieces of diagnostic sherds, of which only 36 were coastal (.7%). The Crystal House had 1,118 diagnostic sherds, of which only 10 were coastal (.9%). A total of 1,442 diagnostic sherds were recovered at the Reception Platform and almost a fourth of those sherds (n = 324, 22.5%) was of the coastal style (see also Tsai 2012a:Table 5.3). This substantial proportion of coastal-style pottery suggests that the Reception Platform, located next to the western entrance of the site (toward the ocean), was likely to have been the first place to receive pottery from persons arriving from the coast.

In sum, evidence for the ritual function of the Reception Platform includes

Architectural plan distinguishing the platform from the residences

(1) T-shaped walls and quincha walls projecting from a central bench
(2) three construction phases, with drastic changes in each phase

Architectural elements not present in the residences

(3) centrally placed bench and bins
(4) circular depressions for holding vessels (pot rests)
(5) storerooms
(6) well-made floor
(7) adobes
(8) clean gravel covering Bench 1

Unique objects or higher percentage of certain artifacts

(9) square dedicatory stone
(10) human phalanx
(11) highest percentage of *Polinices uber*
(12) high percentage of coastal-style pottery relative to the residences

TABLE 5.1. NUMBER OF COASTAL-STYLE DIAGNOSTIC SHERDS FOUND AT LAS VARAS

Location	Coastal-style sherds (n)	%
Reception Platform	324	81
Llama House	36	9
Lambayeque Cemetery	13	3.25
Crystal House	10	2.5
Sector 1, Terrace 2	6	1.5
House 3C	5	1.25
Plazas of the Malquis	4	1
Cemetery of Standing Stones	2	.5
Total	400	100

The Reception Platform would have been the first structure seen by visitors entering from the west. Instead of walking directly into people's houses, the visitors had to pass through the Reception Platform and, in some cases, leave behind their coastal products. In addition, the ritual performed at the platform provided a protocol for the interaction between local residents and their guests from the lower valley; it served as a kind of checkpoint or "welcome center." Most crucially, the identity of an outside ethnic group would have been recognized at the Reception Platform.

THE PLAZAS OF MALQUIS

At the southern end of Las Varas is a hill more than 200 m high, and north of this hill, at its base, are three plazas—the Plazas of Malquis (Figure 5.8). The plazas are placed along a north-south axis with the largest plaza (Plaza 1) situated at the northern end and the smallest plaza (Plaza 3) at the southern end. Standing in Plaza 3 and facing the hill, one would see to the right, the Cemetery of Standing Stones, and to the left, a path that takes one behind the hill into the Quebrada del Caracol, which forms a natural route to the highlands of Trinidad and Contumazá.

Plazas 1 and 2 are lined with single courses of stones, whereas Plaza 3 is a low platform made from stone and mud mortar. The plazas rise in elevation as one proceeds south (Plaza 3 is the highest), and they are connected by benches that serve as steps, allowing access from one plaza to another. This sequence of plaza-bench-plaza repeats until it reaches the southern end of Plaza 3, culminating in a 50-cm-high bench with cist tombs.

Compared to other sectors of Las Varas, at the Plazas of Malquis we excavated only a small area (24 m^2). Empty cists were present on the surface of

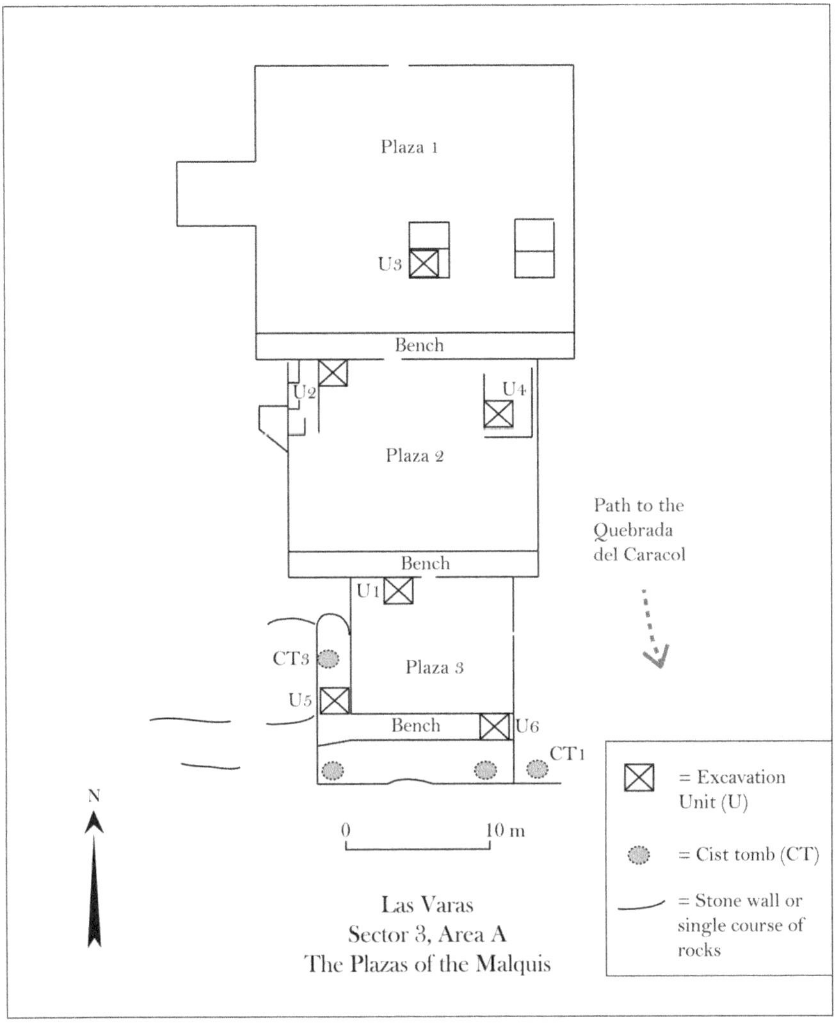

Figure 5.8. Plan of the Plazas of the Malquis, Las Varas. (Courtesy of Howard Tsai)

Plaza 3, so we excavated them to determine whether these cists were tombs or storage pits. I also wanted to investigate the activities associated with these plazas, which—given their large size and unique layout—were presumably used for ritual and ceremony.

I named this sector "Plazas of Malquis"—*malqui* being the Quechua word for "ancestor"—because I believe the cist tombs once held the bones of venerated individuals. No more than 10 cist tombs were found at Las Varas, and most were concentrated at the Plazas of Malquis. Doyle (1988:94) noted that "hundreds of mummies and burial scenes are described in the [ethnohistorical] documents, but only a relatively small percentage of these are said to be malquis." Given the low number of cist tombs at Las Varas, it is likely that individuals placed in the cists were accorded "malqui" status.

Excavation of the Plazas

We excavated Unit 1, a 2 × 2 m square, to define the northern edge of Plaza 3. Patches of ash were found 5 cm below the present surface, and below those patches was a 5-cm-thick layer of guinea pig dung. A few fragments of pottery and marine shell (*Protothaca*) were found in Unit 1.

Unit 2 was placed near the northern edge of Plaza 2, where four fragments of highland Cajamarca-style pottery were found less than 10 cm below the surface. On both the interior and exterior surfaces of these sherds were curvilinear and circular designs in red and black painted over a white background (Figure 5.9). These Cajamarca-style ceramic fragments were not made from kaolin.

Units 3 and 4 were excavated to determine the function of some rectangular structures inside the plazas. These "structures," measuring 2.5 × 4 m, did not appear to be rooms since they consisted of only a single course of stones. Unit 3, placed in one of the two rectangular structures in Plaza 1, produced some marine shells (*Semele* and *Donax*), potsherds, and a small crystal bar. The excavation of Unit 4 produced a few potsherds, chipped stone, bones, and quartz. Very few artifacts or features were found in Units 3 and 4; thus we were unable to determine the function of the rectangular structures.

Units 5 and 6 were placed on the benches west and south of Plaza 3. A small fragment of *Spondylus* was found in Unit 5, and 10–20 cm below the *Spondylus* was a stone post. The presence of the stone post suggests that the plaza was once roofed, though we did not find fragments of wall daub like those found at the Crystal House. Other artifacts from Unit 5 include small quantities of pottery and animal bones.

The excavation of Unit 6 gave us information on the size and construction of the south bench of Plaza 3 (Figure 5.10). This bench is 50 cm high and consists of a retaining wall made from stone and mud mortar. Its upper surface was compact but not hard or smooth enough to be classified as a clay floor. In fact, none of the excavation units in the plazas revealed well-prepared floors like those found at the Reception Platform. Artifacts from Unit 6 include small quantities of potsherds, animal bones, and guinea pig dung.

Unlike the Reception Platform, the Plazas of the Malquis did not have major episodes of remodeling: below most walls and benches of the plazas was sterile soil. If remodeling had occurred, new architectural units were likely built adja-

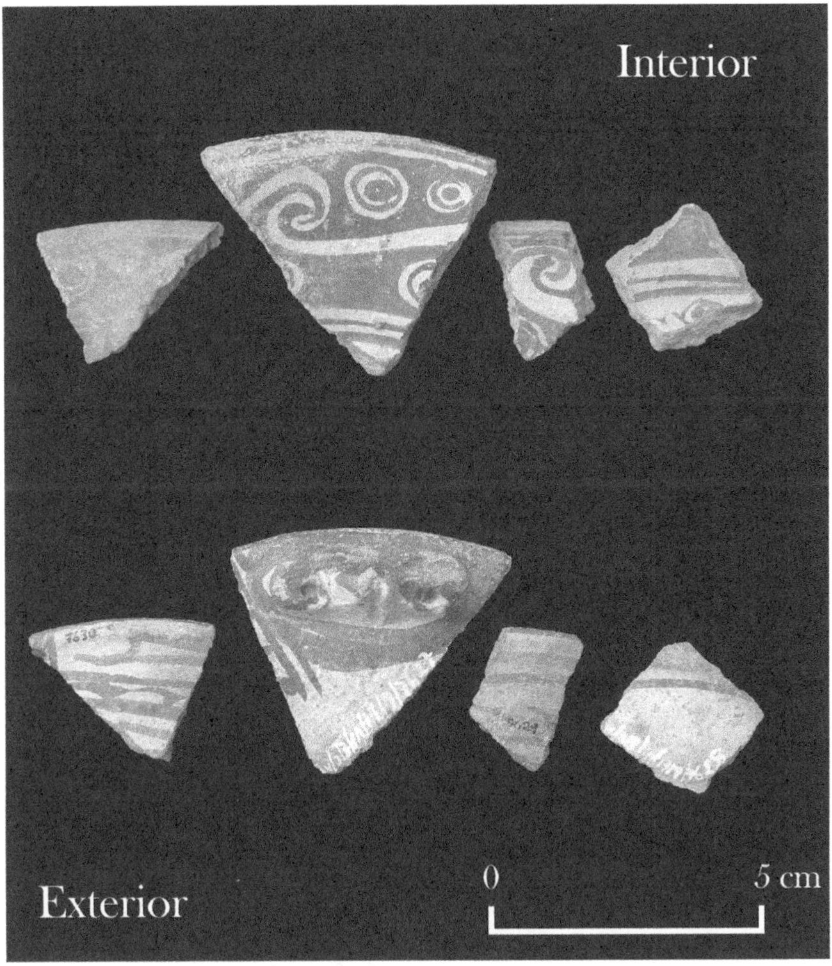

Figure 5.9. Cajamarca-style pottery from Unit 2, Plaza 2, Las Varas. (Courtesy of Howard Tsai)

cent to previous walls or benches rather than above. In other words, the plazas and benches had expanded horizontally rather than vertically like the Reception Platform.

Excavation of Cist Tombs

Four cist tombs have been identified on the benches above Plaza 3 (Figure 5.10), though only one of them—Cist Tomb 3—was excavated. Two more cist tombs (Cist Tombs 1 and 2) are located in the hillside 20 m southeast of Unit 6, and fu-

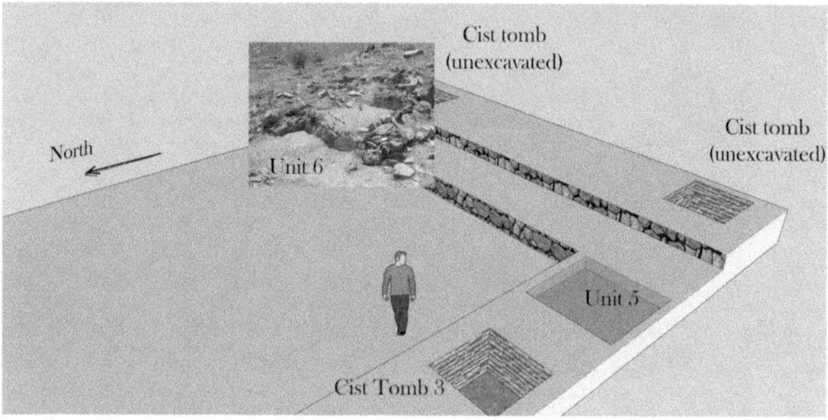

Figure 5.10. Reconstruction of Plaza 3, Las Varas. Unexcavated cist tombs are not assigned numbers, and a fourth cist tomb, east of Unit 6, is not shown. Unit 5 measures 2 × 2 m. (Courtesy of Howard Tsai)

Figure 5.11. Cist Tomb 1, Plazas of the Malquis, Las Varas. It is approximately 1 m deep and 1.5 m wide. (Courtesy of Howard Tsai)

Figure 5.12. Cist tomb labeled as "chulpa" in a park in the highland town of Contumazá, 48 km east of Las Varas. (Courtesy of Howard Tsai)

ture excavations will likely reveal more cist tombs in the area. While Cist Tombs 1 and 2 are oval in shape, Cist Tomb 3 is rectangular with slightly rounded corners. Cist Tomb 1 (Figure 5.11) had been emptied, perhaps by looters, prior to our investigation. We left it unexcavated and, to prevent further damage and looting, we backfilled the tomb. Only Cist Tombs 2 and 3 were excavated for this project.

Cist tombs are a common archaeological feature in the highlands of Peru, including Cajamarca (D. Julien 1988:136–138), Junín (Parsons et al. 2000:172–175), Ayacucho (W. Isbell 2004:9–10), and Cusco (Zapata Rodríguez 1997). They have also been documented in the Moquegua Valley (Goldstein 2005:245–247) and on the coast of the Cañete Valley at the site of Cerro Azul (Marcus 2008b:308–312). In northern Peru, cist tombs are prevalent in the highlands but not on the coast (Figure 5.12). In the Jequetepeque Valley, I have not seen any cist tombs west of Las Varas except for a small cemetery about a kilometer west of the site. The area around Las Varas, therefore, represents the western limit of cist tomb distribution within the valley.

Figure 5.13. Cist Tomb 2, Plazas of the Malquis, Las Varas. Scale, 1 m. (Courtesy of Howard Tsai)

Cist Tomb 1 is an oval, stone-lined pit that measures approximately 1 m deep and 1.5 m wide. The walls of the tomb consist of angular stones stacked together to form a rounded interior. We backfilled Cist Tomb 1 without excavating it, so we do not know whether it was plastered at the bottom.

Cist Tomb 2 is very different from Cist Tomb 1 in construction. Instead of using rectangular stones, the wall of the pit is made entirely of flagstones bound by mud mortar (Figure 5.13). Cist Tomb 2 is the only example of this construction technique at Las Varas, though future excavations might reveal more tombs built in this fashion. The bottom of Cist Tomb 2 is paved with flagstones, and below the flagstones is bedrock. Small fragments of bones, too broken to be identified, were found in Cist Tomb 2. Since we did not find clear evidence of human remains, this structure could have been a storage pit instead of a burial. But if Cist Tomb 2 was indeed a burial pit, it would represent another way of making cist tombs at Las Varas.

Located on the west bench of Plaza 3, Cist Tomb 3 was found filled with stones prior to our excavation. These stones appeared to have been dismantled or have fallen from the north wall of the pit. After removing the collapse, we found

Figure 5.14. Cist Tomb 3, Plazas of the Malquis, Las Varas. The north arrow points to the remains of a human foot. Scale, 1 m. (Courtesy of Howard Tsai)

a layer paved with five flagstones, and beneath this layer of flagstones we found the remains of a human foot (Figure 5.14). The foot rested on a layer of floor that had cane imprints on its underside. Cist Tomb 3 was therefore built on a foundation of large cane stalks with each stalk measuring approximately 4 cm in diameter and oriented north-south. A floor was then plastered over this layer of cane, and human bone was placed above the floor. Besides the human foot, other artifacts in Cist Tomb 3 included small quantities of ceramic sherds.

Three general observations can be made from our excavation of the cist tombs. First, Cist Tomb 3 provides clear evidence for the funerary function of these stone-lined pits, though there is still a chance that other pits were used for storage. Second, the few cist tombs we found in Plaza 3 could not have contained the many generations of people living and dying at Las Varas. Their remains, when piled together, would have made a small mountain of bones. It is more likely that only select individuals, such as the leaders of a lineage or ayllu, were placed in the cist tombs around Plaza 3. Not-so-special individuals were probably interred in the Cemetery of Standing Stones (Sector 2; Tsai 2012a:102–103) or in a small hill overlooking the Lambayeque Cemetery (Sector 4; Tsai 2012a:103–107). At other sites in the Middle Jequetepeque Valley, human remains were placed in caves like those near the town of Santa Catalina in the Quebrada Chausis, some 17 km east of Las Varas.

Finally, our excavations revealed different ways of building cist tombs at Las Varas. Cist Tombs 1 and 2 are oval, whereas Cist Tomb 3 is rectangular. Cist Tombs 1 and 3 were made from stacking rectangular stones, whereas Cist Tomb 2 was made by paving flagstones. Future excavations of cist tombs might reveal a correlation between the shape of the cist with the age, status, or gender of the interred individual. For example, rectangular cist tombs might have contained men, while women were interred in oval pits. A larger sample of excavated cist tombs is needed to give us a better understanding of chaupiyunga burial practices.

Early Spanish Accounts of Andean Plazas

Spanish chroniclers gave us detailed descriptions of Andean plazas in which they disapproved of the amount of idolatry and binge drinking happening at pagan parties. Cieza de León (1959 [1553]:94), for example, recorded the use of plazas in Cajamarca during the sixteenth century: "And when they observed their feasts, a great multitude of people assembled in the clean, well-swept squares, where they performed dances with no small quantity of their wine, brewed from corn and other roots, consumed." From the province of Huamachucho, south of Cajamarca, the Augustinian friars noted that "in these plazas they make great fiestas of their sacrifices that last five days and they make great dances and songs, dressed in their best clothes, and there is great drunkenness, and all this time they never stop drinking, some falling down as others are getting up" (Agustinos 1992 [1560]:15, cited and translated in Moore 1996b:792).

The presence of malquis near plazas was recorded in a seventeenth-century extirpation document from Cajatambo, some 420 km south of Cajamarca: "They discovered a large simulacre and temple from pagan times that had a small plaza and many small rooms all around it, and in the middle three tombs enclosed by stone walls, and they opened and dug up the middle one and showed the idol called Auca Atama, which was a corpse of a pagan individual whom the Indians of this ayllus [Chamas] and those of Nanis adored because he was their first progenitor and conqueror and founder of that town" (Doyle 1988:130).

Even without these Spanish documents, the ritual function of Las Varas's plazas could be proven using only the archaeological evidence. First, the size of the three plazas, being much larger than that of the residences, is an indication that they were used for public events. Second, these plazas are associated with cist tombs, another feature absent from residences. Lastly, many of the rim sherds recovered in the plazas appeared to have been large vessels or cauldrons used for brewing and storing *chicha* (maize beer). The presence of these prehispanic kegs is another indication that feasting and celebration occurred in this area. Only a few excavation units, however, were opened at the Plazas of Malquis; thus more investigation is needed to fully document their construction and associated activities.

Rituals and Boundaries

The differences between the Reception Platform and the Plazas of Malquis are as follows:

(1) Location: The Reception Platform was located at the entrance toward the coast, whereas the Plazas of the Malquis was next to the road to the highlands.

(2) Ampleness: The Plazas of the Malquis was spacious, whereas the Reception Platform had a restricted area.

(3) Renovation: The Reception Platform had undergone several phases of remodeling, whereas the Plazas of Malquis did not experience drastic changes in layout.

(4) No burial was found at the Reception Platform, whereas cist tombs surround the southernmost plaza (Plaza 3) of the Plazas of the Malquis.

Was Las Varas an isolated case of Andeans ritually defining community boundary? In fact, a similar example, where people of a certain gender or ethnicity had to go through designated entrances, was recorded in Huacho during the seventeenth century:

> The site is on one side of the port of Herradura, two and a half leagues [10.5 km] from the town of Huacho, where the sea hits the Playa Chica and bends, and that is why it is called the "horseshoe." . . . The temple lies on a low hill, on the right hand side of the *camino real* [royal road]; the traveler begins to walk, entering this temple by a narrow pathway of walls built on either side, handmade of stone and mud, well and very carefully formed; it is more than a city block long and one enters the temple, which is also walled and made of the same material as the pathway, by different compartments and divisions, some that serve for those from highlands (*serranos*) and others that serve for those from the lowlands (*yungas*), and for the women of these (two regions) there are also different entrances . . . (Medina 1904 [1650]:215, my own translation in the beginning and then translation from Cummins 2008:299 starting at "horseshoe")

Future investigations of this temple near Huacho, by revealing the "different entrances" serving serranos and yungas, would make a great comparative case in light of our results from Las Varas. A possible candidate for Medina's temple is Choque Ispana, located some 12 km south of Huacho (Ruiz Estrada 2006).

A survey of the Upper Mantaro and Tarma drainages by Parsons et al. (2000: 168) had recorded tombs that were placed near the outer walls of settlements. The authors then inferred a relationship between ritual and community boundary: "We suggest that the close spatial association at these settlements between external walls and tomb complexes relates to the importance of public rituals associated with ancestor cults in defining and validating the settlements' larger societal role. The combination of walls and tombs in this highly visible and strategic 'edge' or 'border' setting provided a powerful physical symbol, vis-à-vis comparable social units, of the social distinction of the settlement and of its long-term associations with the immediate area." Ritual was also used to demarcate sacred boundaries by the Incas, an example being the Citua ceremony in which runners passed off ceremonial weapons at designated points some 15 km north, south, west, and east of Cusco (Covey 2006:210).

Andean rituals of marking boundary continued into the twentieth century. Bastien (1978) documented the "New Earth" ritual performed by the highland community of Kaata in Bolivia. In this ritual, people gathered in the courtyard of Sarito, "the one who knows." Here, Sarito would send emissaries to "feed" the earth shrines—that is, put offerings of coca and llama fat into an opening in the ground. These holes or earth shrines were usually covered with rocks and only opened during the time of feeding. Two shrines, Qowila and Kalla Kalla, were "interayllu ritual sites" where members of different ayllus would interact and exchange products such as fruits, pots, bread, and charqui (Bastien 1978:67). By feeding the various earth shrines, the New Earth ritual symbolically united the various body parts of the mountain, including its hands, legs, eyes, etc., into one complete body. This rite reinforced the ties between different communities (Bastien 1978:81) and, like the Inca Citua ceremony, used ritual journey to define the community's boundary.

A similar phenomenon was recorded by Billie Jean Isbell (1978) in the highlands of Ayacucho in September 1970. During the Yaqar Aspiy ritual, a procession traveled from the *sallqa*, the high-altitude pasture, to the *quichwa*, the lower agricultural zone. This journey symbolized the fertilization of the earth, Pachamama, by the mountain spirit, Wamani. The procession would stop at various chapels to make offerings of chicha and coca. These chapels formed concentric rings around the village, and each ring of chapels represented the boundary between the village, sallqa, and quichwa (B. Isbell 1978, Map 5). Isbell argues that this ritual and others reinforced the community's boundary: "The three rituals [the Yarqa Aspiy, Santa Cruz, and the Herranza] embody the concepts of closed, bounded social space dichotomized as civilized (the village) and savage (the sallqa). . . . These three rituals remind the Chuschinos that their society is socially and spatially closed and bounded" (B. Isbell 1978:164).

The ethnographies I have cited show a general relationship between ritual and social boundary, but each case features a different rite or ceremony. Indeed, various rituals may differ in their content but at the end serve the same social function. The use of ritual to define social boundaries is not specific to the Andes. There are many examples of ritual reinforcing (and contesting) social and ethnic identities in other parts of the world (cf. Como 2008; Driessen 1992; Pleck 2000), and a research project could be designed to investigate the long-term effects of ritual on the emergence and evolution of various ethnic groups and their boundaries.

Ritual Boundary and Ethnic Identity

Excavations at the Reception Platform and the Plazas of Malquis revealed an important relationship between ethnicity, ritual, and public space. First, interaction between different ethnic groups occurred in the ritual or public area. Las Varas, located between the coast and the highlands, received products from both regions. Visitors or traders did not walk directly into people's houses. Instead, their arrival and traffic flow were channeled by ritual structures built near Las Varas's entrances. These "checkpoints" guided the interaction between locals and outsiders.

Differences between the two ritual areas led to a difference in treatment between coastal and highland communities. The Reception Platform was much smaller than the Plazas of Malquis, and therefore it restricted the number of visitors who entered from the coast. People arriving from the highlands, by contrast, would enter spacious plazas surrounded by cist tombs. Coastal visitors could see those plazas only from a distance when they first entered Las Varas. These coastal people might advance further and see the Plazas of Malquis and participate in the fiestas, and vice versa; the highlanders might go farther west and tour the Reception Platform. But an outsider visiting Las Varas for the first time would need to go through one of the two checkpoints, each with a unique reception area, depending on whether one came from the coast or the highlands.

The implication is that ritual or public space, for example, a ceremonial plaza, was an important locale where people recognized and reinforced their ethnic identities. In the previous chapter, I noted that the excavation of houses could provide data on the material culture of a particular ethnic group. It is in the public sphere, however, that people share their ideas on religion, gender, ethnicity, and politics with other families or communities, forming the "distinction" of taste—Bourdieu's habitus (discussed in chapter 1)—that ultimately leads to their decision to join or leave certain groups. Thus it benefits archaeologists that the activities and material remains associated with public areas are different from those found in the house. By excavating multiple contexts, such as houses, plazas, and cemeteries, and by assessing the differences between these data sets, we can arrive at a clearer picture of boundary-making and better explain the construction of ethnic identity.

6

An Archaeological Investigation of Ethnicity

Results from Las Varas provide new archaeological information and theoretical understanding on three levels: first, we have identified a local chaupiyunga culture in the Middle Jequetepeque Valley with its own ceramic and architectural styles. Second, we see that the chaupiyunga community of Las Varas engaged in at least two modes of economic strategy—exchange and colonization—rather than relying solely on the "vertical archipelago." Third, on the broadest theoretical level, the entrances of Las Varas illustrate the importance of ritual in forming ethnic boundaries and creating a protocol for inter-ethnic interaction.

Las Varas and Its Chaupiyunga Material Culture

Excavations in the residential sector uncovered domestic objects such as cooking pots, stone jambs, and spindle whorls that served as "proxies" for the ethnic affiliation of Las Varas households. These features and artifacts were evidence of everyday activities: hearths for cooking, whorls for spinning, and pens for keeping guinea pigs. Residents of Las Varas used a style of pottery that, originating from the middle valley (chaupiyunga), was distinct from those of the coast and the highlands.

We excavated two ritual areas located near the west and south entrances of Las Varas. Near the west entrance, which faced the coast, we found a ritual platform that had large quantities of coastal-style pottery; this suggests that coastal people arrived at the platform and traded with the residents of Las Varas. The other ritual area was a series of plazas located near the south entrance, which faced the highlands. One plaza was surrounded by cist tombs, a type of burial structure commonly found in the highlands.

Excavations in the ritual areas of Las Varas gave us another view of ethnic interaction. The ritual areas showed that the community of Las Varas received highland and coastal visitors at different entrances. Coastal visitors entered via a ritual platform, whereas highlanders entered via ceremonial plazas. This indicates that ethnic differences were perceived at Las Varas and that public rituals served to reinforce different identities.

Jequetepeque Valley, AD 800–1200

Data from Las Varas allow us to reconstruct the cultural history of the Jequetepeque Valley from the end of the Middle Horizon to the first half of the Late Intermediate. During the Late Moche period (AD 600–800), Cajamarca-style pottery began appearing on coastal Moche sites like Huaca Colorada (Swenson et al. 2011:120, 123) and San José de Moro (Bernuy and Bernal 2008). At San José de Moro, excavations of Late Moche, Transitional, and Lambayeque burials allowed Bernuy and Bernal (2008:73–75) to devise a chronology of Coastal Cajamarca bowls. Painted inside the earliest Coastal Cajamarca bowls, recovered from Late Moche (AD 600–800) and Transitional (AD 800–900) burials, was a wavy red line that spiraled out, like a coil, from the center (Figure 4.23) (Bernuy and Bernal 2008:Cuadro 2). Only a few fragments of this wavy-line bowl were found at Las Varas.

After the wavy-line design came the satellite motif, which appeared in the Late Transitional (ca. AD 900) tombs of San José de Moro (Bernuy and Bernal 2008:74). The last phase of the Coastal Cajamarca tradition (after AD 1000), exemplified by bowls from Las Varas, saw a proliferation of motifs including animals (crab, llama, fox), checkerboard, volute, concentric circles, and so on.

Only the last two phases of Coastal Cajamarca or chaupiyunga-style bowls were found at Las Varas. This indicates that, around AD 900–1000, a community from the chaupiyunga had migrated toward the coast, eventually settling at Las Varas. These migrants brought with them their architectural canon (terraced residences and stone jambs), burial tradition (cist tombs), and pottery style (everted jars and painted bowls). Since no earlier occupation was found at Las Varas, they most likely arrived at an empty or near-empty patch of land. If my hypothesis concerning this migration is correct, we should find sites to the east of Las Varas with wavy-line bowls that date earlier than AD 900.

Las Varas had a powerful neighbor: Ventanillas. Las Varas and Ventanillas seemed to have engaged in peaceful exchange, as we found chaupiyunga pottery in Ventanillas and coastal pottery in Las Varas. We did not find any fortification at Las Varas, and such evidence for warfare, like Moche hilltop forts replete with defensive walls, parapets, and sling stones, is prevalent on the coast (Dillehay 2001:271–272). Despite the apparently friendly relationship between Las Varas and Ventanillas, their interaction was restricted or mediated, as evidenced by the construction of the Reception Platform, to control the flow of visitors from coastal communities. Interestingly, many sites with coastal pottery and architecture were located up-valley from Las Varas (Ravines 1982), which meant that chaupiyunga and coastal communities had permeable or semi-permeable boundaries allowing them to bypass each other's territory.

It is unclear when Las Varas was abandoned. The Llama House was the earliest structure at Las Varas, as indicated by radiocarbon dating and associated pottery, and the Crystal House and Reception Platform were occupied somewhat later. During its abandonment, the Llama House was offered three painted bowls that were then covered with midden and ash. The Crystal House received no such goodbye ceremony—its walls were left to weather, decay, and collapse. Pottery from the last construction phase of the Reception Platform suggests that Las Varas was abandoned around AD 1300; this is a speculative assessment that needs to be tested by more radiocarbon samples.

Mixed Economy: Colonization and Exchange

In chapter 3, I described Murra's vertical archipelago (colonization) model as one strategy to acquire distant resources. If indeed Las Varas was settled by chaupiyunga people from the east, then it appears that two strategies—colonization and exchange—were employed. Cieza de León (1959 [1553]:321–322) noted that, out of all the coastal valleys he had visited, the Pacasmayo (Jequetepeque) Valley was the "most fertile and thickly settled." Cieza's statement would imply that, in the centuries and millennia before European contact, the valley was being gradually filled with people and settlements, such as when a group of chaupiyunga migrants moved downriver and established a village at Las Varas.

The inhabitants of Las Varas were able to acquire coastal resources (shellfish), but how? Did they trade with coastal fishermen, or did they go to the coast and bring seafood back to Las Varas? Since the purpose of the Reception Platform was to filter visitors, it is therefore more likely that Las Varas had traded with coastal communities, because if everyone entering Las Varas was from the community itself, then it would not have been necessary to create a designated entrance like the Reception Platform. Given the long stretch of chaupiyunga land in the Jequetepeque Valley, mid-valley communities must have been the middlemen in coast-highland exchange and interaction.

Ancient Andeans, like their descendents today, would have acquired resources in many different ways, including pilgrimage, regular visits to friends and families, and offering their labor in exchange for goods. Let us imagine, then, that several families from Las Varas are going upvalley to help their friends harvest coca, after which they get to keep a few bags filled with leaves for themselves. They then head down to the coast to participate in a ceremony, exchanging coca and nicely painted bowls for fish and seafood, and return to Las Varas, along with some friends from the coast, where they engage in more exchange at the

Reception Platform. Such small-scale, yet regular and important movements of people and goods do not create archaeologically identifiable ethnic settlements or neighborhoods. In other words, none of these activities would show up as an intrusive colony in the archaeological record.

Decades of archaeological, ethnohistorical, and ethnographic research have revealed the variety and diversity of economic strategies available to Andean communities, ranging from the intrusive colonies of states and empires (Wari and Tiwanaku) to mere cohabitation of different ayllus and ethnic groups within one village (documented in the visitas of Cajamarca and Chucuito). It is unlikely that Murra's vertical archipelago had been the only mode of resource exploitation among prehispanic Andean communities. Brush (1977:10–16) argues that in long, extended valleys with gradual slopes, communities would tend to specialize and exchange their products. By contrast, when a valley has a steep slope, its many ecological floors will be compressed in a smaller area, and therefore communities would directly colonize and exploit different altitudinal zones. Perhaps because of its length and gradual slope, the Jequetepeque Valley fostered communities that traded or, like Las Varas, employed a mixed strategy of trade *and* colonization. A third possible strategy, described by Dillehay (1976:407–411) and Rostworowski de Diez Canseco (1977:186), was labor-for-produce exchange: laborers being rewarded with agricultural products in exchange for helping with the harvest.

In sum, Mayer (2002:58) notes that "no economic system is as pure as the models that scholars construct." If so, what we see in the archaeological record is a mash-up of materials, like an overcooked stew, that represent a blend of diverse cultural and economic strategies. Our challenge, then, is to identify the individual ingredients and decipher their proportions from a morass of archaeological remains.

Ritual, Boundary, Information

The result from Las Varas and its theoretical significance can now be situated within previous anthropological studies on ethnicity (chapter 1):

1. There is no natural or inevitable packaging of language, culture, social organization, and other traits into a coherent and impermeable "ethnic group." Individuals may change their identity (easier said than done), and new identities appear and replace old ones.

2. Nevertheless, as Barth has pointed out, ethnic divides persist even as intermarriage and trade push people and goods across boundaries. The challenge for archaeologists, then, is to identify the processes responsible for creating ethnic boundaries.

3. At Las Varas, ritual was a mechanism by which ethnic differences were constructed. The importance of ritual in defining ethnic and social boundaries is documented in many ethnohistorical and ethnographic cases in the Andes (chapter 5); a survey of anthropological studies from other parts of the world might reveal more examples of ritual reinforcing ethnicity.

4. Ritual's effectiveness in maintaining ethnic boundaries is explained by Rappaport's theory of "digitization," which states that ritual creates clear-cut, black/white ("digital") signals of difference, resulting in clear lines of demarcation between social groups. Rappaport applied his framework to explain the conferral of age, clan, gender, and other types of social membership during rituals. In the case of Las Varas, I argue that ritual's discretizing or digitizing effect served to recognize the distinctiveness of ethnic groups.

Ethnic identities are created by contrasts with the "other." The investigation of ethnicity, then, is necessarily an elucidation of the *relation* between two or more groups. Instead of approaching ethnicity as "A does this and B does that," we should examine what happens "when A meets B." This framework, focusing on relations, can be extended to investigations of other kinds of social categories such as gender and class. For instance, an archaeological study of gender should examine the mutual feedback of self- and other-construction between various gendered categories. The formation of class does not occur in separate spheres—the poor did not choose to become a lower class on their own, nor did the rich maintain their status by merely keeping to themselves. At some point the classes have to meet and interact, and it is at this moment of articulation that class relations form. In ancient civilizations, the site of monumental construction is one such area where class relationship becomes clear: here the labor-contributing class is administered by their overseers who will live and rule from the very buildings the workers erect.

Interactions between unequals are structured by protocols. When different ethnic groups interact, new rules must be introduced because the parties have different ideas about what is proper or correct. This interethnic protocol is analogous to a pidgin language developed to facilitate communication between speakers of different languages. An illustrative example, provided by Leach (1954:220–221), demonstrates the creative fudging of rules when Shans marry Kachins. The Kachin marriage system ranks the wife-giving clan as higher than the bride-receiving clan. By contrast, Shan princes frequently receive brides from lower-ranking subjects. A cultural conundrum arises, then, when a Shan prince marries a Kachin high-ranking lady, or when a male Kachin chief marries a female Shan commoner—who shall rise in rank as a result of the marriage?

The solution is the creation of a special "blood brotherhood" that puts the partners on equal footing, elevating neither the bride's nor the groom's family in relative status (Leach 1954:220–221). In some cases, however, both parties can agree on a patron-client relationship, such as when a Shan noble or Kachin chief marries a commoner or when a Kachin chief marries a Shan princess and submits to Shan overlordship.

Such special, interethnic protocols could result from either careful deliberation or hasty improvisation. Diplomatic arrangements made at the border or frontier must have been a common feature as ethnic groups are brought into contact; they ensure a structured relationship that is repeated, predictable, and ritualized. As discussed in chapter 5, the ritual areas of Las Varas provided the protocol and arena for structuring interaction between ethnic groups. At the Reception Platform, the frequency of renovation or remodeling is suggestive of an unstable relationship—constantly changing protocols—between the coast and the chaupiyunga.

The Multicontextual Approach

At the end of chapter 4, I questioned the utility of the single-context approach, which prefers one particular archaeological context over another for investigating ethnicity. Since identities are relational and created during interactions, no single social arena can thus encompass all society's categories. Ethnic identity, like any other identity (gender, class, age, profession), manifests itself differently depending on the context. Foreigners abroad, for example, represent their nation, but back at home they are tied up with the country's internal divisions and politics.

Context affects the meaning of an interaction. A conversation over the dinner table is different from a discussion at a town hall, even if those conversations involve the same words. Rappaport (1999:15) asserted the elevated truthfulness (or rather, reduced falsehood) of information when it was conveyed during ritual, and this relationship between the context of performance and its meaning has great implications for understanding practice and material culture. Because of the importance of context in determining meaning, we cannot divorce a certain activity, object, or symbol from the setting in which it was employed. Indeed this is *the* central tenet of archaeology: the cultural meaning and scientific significance of archaeological findings derive only from their spatial relation to other archaeological sites, features, and artifacts.

The importance of a multicontextual approach was made clear at Las Varas. Data from the various sectors of Las Varas, when combined, provided a crucial synthesis for understanding the process of ethnic interaction. Had we not excavated the residential sectors, I would not have understood how domestic architecture and pottery at Las Varas differed from those of the coast. Had we not excavated the ritual sectors, I would not have realized how ritual played a key role in enforcing ethnic identities. Only by excavating both the domestic and ritual contexts was I able to demonstrate how ethnic categories had been manifested and performed in private and public spaces.

Hence, for archaeologists investigating ethnicity, it would be best to excavate multiple contexts: houses, burials, public areas, palaces, fortifications, and so on. Another recommendation would be to zoom out and examine variability at different scales, at the level of the household, neighborhood, site, and region. Sharp differences in style between adjacent houses, communities, or regions are suggestive of ethnic differences, but, lest we fall back on Kossinna's paradigm, we must demonstrate that these groups interacted with each other and that they had indeed made and maintained ethnic boundaries.

The Strategic Emergence of Structure

As discussed in chapter 1, Leach, Barth, and Bourdieu all noted the importance of strategy in modeling cultural decisions, with Barth applying game theory to his study of Pathan alliance formation. Yet 60 years after Barth's innovative approach, game theory has just about disappeared from sociocultural anthropology, probably because most ethnographers, fearing the specter of determinism, turned away from quantitative analysis (the preferred tool of environmental determinists or materialists) and opted for qualitative explanations based on cultural logic or structure. The irony is that cultural explanations, in accounting for events or processes a posteriori, can be just as deterministic as, if not more than, ecological or economic factors. If something had happened because and only because of cultural-structural principles, then such rules have a death grip on human action, dictating regular and 100% predictable behavior.

Game theory, counterintuitively, allows an escape from deterministic paradigms. Models in game theory, in considering the rules and constraints of strategic decisions, can reveal contingent, creative, and idiosyncratic actions. Only in rare occasions can the outcome of the game be predicted with certainty (as in the Nash Equilibrium), but most of the time each game is played out differently, like chess. Players vary in their competence and skill, but ultimately an innovative solution, a competitive edge, can tip over the structural deadlock of a standoff, turning peer competition into hierarchical integration, irreversibly altering the geopolitical landscape. Were we to identify such a transformative moment, we would be discovering an ideal instance of agency: actions that follow cultural rules but, being uniquely and unforeseeably executed, subvert the system.

This is the kind of meaningful event we should be looking for in studying social change, but the paradox is that we cannot understand creative idiosyncrasies without first understanding the rules. And often the rules themselves are born of repeated interactions. An ethnographer, for instance, might record a practice as following some kind of cultural structure or norm. But someone with a long-term perspective, such as a historian or an archaeologist, might realize that it took decades or centuries of interactive decisions, with individuals gaining, losing, and learning to shape that normalized practice as witnessed by the ethnographer. This is emergent structure in the sense of a complex system—the emergence of macrostructure from actors responding to each other's strategic decisions.

Game theory is therefore particularly useful for archaeologists who view long-term history as comprising systemic, interactive feedbacks of decisions and strategies. Take, for example, the increasing use of iron nails in the massive fortified walls—*murus gallicus*—of European Iron Age oppida, which culminated in the nailing of some 300 tons of iron (12,100 nails [Vandemoortele 2011:105]) in the city walls of Manching in Bavaria, Germany. This tremendous investment in iron nails makes sense if we consider the archaeological record: in preceding centuries, many wooden fortifications had been burned down during attacks, and Manching's iron defense was the result of a long-term arms race to protect settlements against flaming arrows or spears (Piggott 1970:216). Oppida after oppida must have been built, sieged, and razed, their inhabitants working harder and harder to procure more iron to forge stronger walls, all the while preoccupied that their neighbors are building not just good but better defenses.

We can now apply game theory to explain certain relations or practices in the Andes. The grueling litigation between the Canta and Chaclla (chapter 2) could be seen as a case of "war of attrition" in which the costs of inflicting damage on one's opponent, despite the cost and effort incurred on oneself, are still low enough to prevent encroachment. Low-level harassments like uprooting crops or removing fieldstones are quick and dirty ways to mess with your opponent's assets. The Late Intermediate saw a proliferation of massive forts and hilltop defenses. Endemic warfare, in addition to population pressure, could lead to disastrous wars of attrition. Population growth confers military advantage to a community but exerts unsustainable pressure on the land and its resources. A growing but territorially bounded community would eat itself from inside out. To avoid this Malthusian tragedy, communities can band together and form a confederation that jointly conducts offensive and defensive operations, thereby breaking the deadlock. Barth's original work on game theory provided a mathematical equation to evaluate the costs and benefits of Pathan alliance formation; we should expect similar kinds of calculation made by ambitious leaders in creating a state or empire. Unless a kingdom has complete military and economic dominance (unlikely in the busy field of peer polities), it will need wily diplomacy, utilizing bribes and brides to build that initial momentum of supremacy and expansion.

In the case of Las Varas, the passing of information via ritual illustrates the importance of expressing sincerity and truth in potentially competitive situations. Ritual was used to mark boundaries, signal information on identity, and set the proper protocols of interaction. Without such mechanisms to sanctify intent, actors would be forever stuck confessing and ratting each other out in the prisoner's dilemma. Ritual essentially allows competing parties to sincerely say, "I will cooperate." There are tremendous costs to not cooperating—your opponents and their allies have just sealed a pact to conduct a joint military campaign while you continue to squabble with your neighbors. Seen in this light, the frequent association of defensive structures with ritual sanctuaries (Arkush and Stanish 2005:11–12; Swenson 2012) is no longer a paradox: the Janus face of conflict and cooperation is flipped by discrete/digital signals of ritual performance. Much pomp and circumstance surround political violence, just as feasts, ceremonies, and sacrifices serve to seal agreements and alliances; they sanctify promises and mete justice, gods willing, for betrayed loyalties.

My suggested application of game theory to Andean prehistory is preliminary and speculative, but I think this line of inquiry has great potential for understanding ritual and ethnicity. Were we to accurately model actors' interactive strategies and reveal emergent structures, we would succeed in surpassing the simple subjective/objective dichotomy Bourdieu had criticized. I hope my investigation of Las Varas can convince archaeologists to reopen the old case file that is ethnicity, but this time we should reexamine issues of interaction and structure in a new theoretical light. Perhaps the Reception Platform and the Plazas of the Malquis represent a unique instance of ethnicized entrances, but I doubt that Las Varas would prove to be the only community in the Andes to have lived differently from its neighbors, established ritual and ethnic boundaries, designed household goods in a fashion distinctive of its homeland, and left all that behind to be discovered, centuries later, by archaeologists wanting to investigate ethnicity, ritual, and strategy.

References Cited

Acosta, José de
2002 [1590] *Natural and Moral History of the Indies*. Translated by Frances M. López Morillas. Duke University Press, Durham.

Adams, E. Charles
1983 The Architectural Analogue to Hopi Social Organization and Room Use, and Implications for Prehistoric Northern Southwestern Culture. *American Antiquity* 48(1):44–61.

Agustinos
1992 [1560] *Relación de la religión y ritos del Perú hecha por los padres agustinos*. Fondo Editorial de la Pontificia Universidad Católica del Perú, Lima.

Albornoz, Cristóbal de
1989 [1580s] Instrucción para descrubrir todas las guacas del piru y sus camayos y haziendas. In *Fábulas y mitos de los incas*, edited by Henrique Urbano and Pierre Duviols, pp. 160–198. Historia 16, Madrid.

Aldenderfer, Mark S. (editor)
1993 *Domestic Architecture, Ethnicity, and Complementarity in the South-Central Andes*. University of Iowa Press, Iowa City.

Allen, Catherine J.
1988 *The Hold Life Has: Coca and Cultural Identity in an Andean Community*. Smithsonian Institution Press, Washington, DC.

Anders, Martha, Susana Arce, Izumi Shimada, Victor Chang, Luis Tokuda, and Sonia Quiroz
1998 Early Middle Horizon Pottery Production at Maymi, Pisco Valley, Peru. In *Andean Ceramics: Technology, Organization, and Approaches*, edited by Izumi Shimada, pp. 233–251. Museum Applied Science Center for Archaeology, University of Pennsylvania Museum of Archaeology and Anthropology, Philadelphia.

Arguedas, José María, and Pierre Duviols
1966 *Dioses y hombres de Huarochirí: Narración quechua recogida por Francisco de Avila [¿1598?]*. Instituto de Estudios Peruanos, Lima.

Arkush, Elizabeth, and Charles Stanish
2005 Interpreting Conflict in the Ancient Andes: Implications for the Archaeology of Warfare. *Current Anthropology* 46(1): 3–28.

Arriaga, Pablo José de

1999 [1621] *La extirpación de la idolatría en el Pirú.* Cuadernos para la historia de la evangelización en América Latina No. 13. Centro de Estudios Regionales Andinos "Bartolomé de Las Casas," Cuzco, Peru.

1968 [1621] *The Extirpation of Idolatry in Peru.* Translated by L. Clark Keating. University of Kentucky Press, Lexington.

Bakhtin, Mikhail Mikhailovich

1981 *The Dialogic Imagination: Four Essays.* Translated by Caryl Emerson and Michael Holquist. University of Texas Press, Austin.

Barazangi, Muawia, and Bryan L. Isacks

1976 Spatial Distribution of Earthquakes and Subduction of the Nazca Plate beneath South America. *Geology* 4:686–692.

Barth, Fredrik

1959 Segmentary Opposition and the Theory of Games: A Study of Pathan Organization. *Journal of the Royal Anthropological Institute of Great Britain and Ireland* 89(1): 5–21.

1969a Introduction. In *Ethnic Groups and Boundaries: The Social Organization of Culture Difference*, edited by Fredrik Barth, pp. 1–38. Little, Brown, Boston.

1969b Pathan Identity and Its Maintenance. In *Ethnic Groups and Boundaries: The Social Organization of Culture Difference*, edited by Fredrik Barth, pp. 117–134. Little, Brown, Boston.

2007 Overview: Sixty Years in Anthropology. *Annual Review of Anthropology* 36:1–16.

Barth, Fredrik (editor)

1969 *Ethnic Groups and Boundaries: The Social Organization of Culture Difference.* Little, Brown, Boston.

Barth, Fredrik, and Robert Anderson

2007 Interview with Fredrik Barth. *Revista de Antropología Iberoamericana* 2(2):i–xvi.

Bastien, Joseph W.

1978 *Mountain of the Condor: Metaphor and Ritual in an Andean Ayllu.* Waveland, Long Grove, Illinois.

Bateson, Gregory

1951 Conventions of Communication: Where Validity Depends on Belief. In *Communication: The Social Matrix of Psychiatry*, edited by Jurgen Ruesch and Gregory Bateson, pp. 212–227. Norton, New York.

Bauer, Brian S.

1998 *The Sacred Landscape of the Inca: The Cusco Ceque System.* University of Texas Press, Austin.

Begler, Elsie B.

1980 *Modernization of Agricultural Production and the Problem of Rural Unemployment: The Search for Work among the Rural Proletariat of the Peruvian North Coast.* PhD dissertation, Colombia University, New York. University Microfilms, Ann Arbor.

Bennett, Wendell C.

1944 *The North Highlands of Peru: Excavations in the Callejon de Huaylas and at Chavin de Huantar.* American Museum of Natural History, New York.

1946 The Archeology of the Central Andes. In *The Andean Civilizations*, edited by Julian H. Steward, pp. 61–147. Handbook of South American Indians, Vol. 2. Smithsonian Institution, Washington, DC.

Bentley, G. Carter

1987 Ethnicity and Practice. *Comparative Studies in Society and History* 29(1):24–55.

Berger, Thomas

1978 *Arthur Rex: A Legendary Novel.* Delacorte/Seymour Lawrence, New York.

Berlin, Isaiah

1976 *Vico and Herder: Two Studies in the History of Ideas.* Hogarth, London.

Bernuy, Katiusha, and Vanessa Bernal

2008 La tradición Cajamarca en San José de Moro: Una evidencia de interacción interregional durante el Horizonte Medio. In *Arqueología mochica: Nuevos enfoques*, edited by Luis Jaime Castillo Butters, Hélène Bernier, Gregory D. Lockard, and Julio Rucabado Yong, pp. 67–80. Fondo Editorial de la Pontificia Universidad Católica del Perú, Lima.

Billman, Brian R.

1996 The Evolution of Prehistoric Political Organizations in the Moche Valley, Peru. PhD dissertation, University of California, Santa Barbara. University Microfilms, Ann Arbor.

2002 Irrigation and the Origins of the Southern Moche State on the North Coast of Peru. *Latin American Antiquity* 13(4):371–400.

Binford, Lewis R.

1962 Archaeology as Anthropology. *American Antiquity* 28(2):217–225.

Bonavia, Duccio

1982 Trabajos efectuados. In *Los Gavilanes: Mar, desierto y oásis en la historia del hombre*, edited by Duccio Bonavia, pp. 25–72. Corporación Financiera de Desarrollo S.A., Lima.

2008 *The South American Camelids.* Translated by Javier Flores Espinoza. Monograph 64. Cotsen Institute of Archaeology, University of California, Los Angeles.

Boswell, Alicia

2016 *Chimú and Inca Frontier Interactions: A Local Study of the Moche Valley Chaupiyunga, North Coast of Perú.* Unpublished PhD dissertation, University of California, San Diego.

Bourdieu, Pierre

1970 La maison kabyle ou le monde renversé. In *Échanges et communications: Mélanges offerts à Claude Lévi-Strauss à l'occasion de son 60ème anniversaire*, Vol. 2, edited by Jean Pouillon and Pierre Maranda, pp. 187–207. Mouton, The Hague.

1977 *Outline of a Theory of Practice.* Translated by Richard Nice. Cambridge University Press, Cambridge.

1984 *Distinction: A Social Critique of the Judgement of Taste.* Translated by Richard Nice. Harvard University Press, Cambridge, Massachusetts.

1990 *The Logic of Practice.* Translated by Richard Nice. Stanford University Press, Stanford.

Bourdieu, Pierre, and Loïc J. D. Wacquant
1992 *An Invitation to Reflexive Sociology*. University of Chicago Press, Chicago.
Brooks, William E., Jason C. Willett, Jonathan D. Kent, Victor Vasquez, and Teresa Rosales
2005 The Muralla Pircada: An Ancient Andean Debris Flow Retention Dam, Santa Rita B archaeological site, Chao Valley, Northern Perú. *Landslides* 2(2):117–123.
Brush, Stephen B.
1977 *Mountain, Field, and Family: The Economy and Human Ecology of an Andean Valley*. University of Pennsylvania Press, Philadelphia.
Buikstra, Jane E.
1995 Tombs for the Living . . . or . . . for the Dead: The Osmore Ancestors. In *Tombs for the Living: Andean Mortuary Practices*, edited by Tom D. Dillehay, pp. 229–280. Dumbarton Oaks Research Library and Collection, Washington, DC.
Burga, Manuel.
1976 *De la encomienda a la hacienda capitalista: El valle del Jequetepeque del siglo XVI al XX*. Instituto de Estudios Peruanos, Lima.
Burger, Richard L.
1992 *Chavin and the Origins of Andean Civilization*. Thames and Hudson, New York.
1998 *Excavaciones en Chavín de Huántar*. Fondo Editorial de la Pontificia Universidad Católica del Perú, Lima.
2008 Chavín de Huántar and Its Sphere of Influence. In *Handbook of South American Archaeology*, edited by Helaine Silverman and William H. Isbell, pp. 681–703. Springer, New York.
Burger, Richard L., and Lucy Salazar Burger
1980 Ritual and Religion at Huaricoto. *Archaeology* 33:26–32.
Burmeister, Stefan
2000 Approaches to an Archaeological Proof of Migration. *Current Anthropology* 41(4):539–567.
Bussmann, Rainer W., and Douglas Sharon
2009 Naming a Phantom: The Quest to Find the Identity of *Ulluchu*, an Unidentified Ceremonial Plant of the Moche Culture in Northern Peru. *Journal of Ethnobiology and Ethnomedicine* 5(1):8.
Cabello Valboa, Miguel
1951 [1586] *Miscelánea antártica: Una historia del Perú antiguo*. Instituto de Etnología, Universidad Nacional Mayor de San Marcos, Lima.
Cahill, Thomas, and Bryan L. Isacks
1992 Seismicity and Shape of the Subducted Nazca Plate. *Journal of Geophysical Research* 97(B12):17503–17529.
Calancha, Antonio de la
1977 [1639] *Corónica moralizada del orden de San Agustín en el Perú*. Vol. 4. Universidad Nacional Mayor de San Marcos, Lima.
Capasso, Luigi, Kenneth A. R. Kennedy, and Cynthia A. Wilczak
1999 *Atlas of Occupational Makers on Human Remains*. Edigrafital S.p.A., Teramo, Italy.

Carneiro, Robert L.

1969 The Measurement of Cultural Development in the Ancient Near East and in Anglo-Saxon England. *Transactions of the New York Academy of Sciences*, Series 2, 31(8):1013–1023.

1981 Herbert Spencer as an Anthropologist. *Journal of Libertarian Studies* 5(2):153–210.

2000 *The Muse of History and the Science of Culture*. Kluwer Academic/Plenum, New York.

2002 The Tribal Village and Its Culture: An Evolutionary Stage in the History of Human Society. In *The Archaeology of Tribal Societies*, edited by William A. Parkinson, pp. 34–52. International Monographs in Prehistory, Ann Arbor.

Castillo, Luis Jaime

2001 The Last of the Mochicas: A View from the Jequetepeque Valley. In *Moche Art and Archaeology in Ancient Peru*, edited by Joanne Pillsbury, pp. 306–332. Yale University Press, New Haven.

2011 *San José de Moro y la arqueología del valle de Jequetepeque*. Fondo Editorial de la Pontificia Universidad Católica del Perú, Lima.

Castillo, Luis Jaime, and Christopher B. Donnan

1994 Los mochica del norte y los mochica del sur. In *Vicús*, edited by Krzysztof Makowski, Christopher B. Donnan, and Iván Amaro Bullón, pp. 143–176. Banco de Crédito del Perú, Lima.

Caviedes, César

2001 *El Niño in History: Storming through the Ages*. University Press of Florida, Gainesville.

Childe, V. Gordon

1927 Review of *Ursprung und Verbreitung der Germanen in vor- und frühgeschichtlicher Zeit*, by Gustaf Kossinna. *Man* 27(33):54–55.

1930 *The Bronze Age*. Cambridge University Press, Cambridge.

1933 Is Prehistory Practical? *Antiquity* 7(28):410–418.

1936 *Man Makes Himself*. Watts, London.

1942 The Significance of Soviet Archæology. *Labour Monthly* 24(11):341–343.

1946 Archaeology and Anthropology. *Southwestern Journal of Anthropology* 2(3):243–251.

1950 The Urban Revolution. *The Town Planning Review* 21(1):3–17.

1958 Retrospect. *Antiquity* 32(126):69–74.

Cieza de León, Pedro de

1959 [1553] *The Incas of Pedro de Cieza de León*. Translated by Harriet de Onis. University of Oklahoma Press, Norman.

1984 [1553] Crónica del Perú. Parte primera. In *Pedro de Cieza de León: Obras completas*, edited by Carmelo Sáenz de Santa María, pp. 1–144. Vol. 1. Consejo Superior de Investigaciones Científicas, Madrid.

2000 [1550s] *El señorío de los Incas*. Dastin, Madrid.

Clarke, Giles
1975 Popular Movements and Late Roman Cemeteries. *World Archaeology* 7(1):46–56.
Cobbing, E. J., and Wally S. Pitcher
1972 Plate Tectonics and the Peruvian Andes. *Nature Physical Science* 240:51–53.
Cobo, Bernabé
1979 [1653] *History of the Inca Empire: An Account of the Indians' Customs and Their Origin, together with a Treatise on Inca Legends, History, and Social Institutions.* Translated by Roland Hamilton. University of Texas Press, Austin.
1990 [1653] *Inca Religion and Customs.* Translated by Roland Hamilton. University of Texas Press, Austin.
Cohen, Ronald
1978 Ethnicity: Problem and Focus in Anthropology. *Annual Review of Anthropology* 7:379–403.
Comaroff, John L.
1987 Of Totemism and Ethnicity: Consciousness, Practice and the Signs of Inequality. *Ethnos* 52(3/4):301–323.
Como, Michael I.
2008 *Shōtoku: Ethnicity, Ritual, and Violence in the Japanese Buddhist Tradition.* Oxford University Press, Oxford.
Cook, David Noble
1981 *Demographic Collapse: Indian Peru, 1520–1620.* Cambridge University Press, Cambridge.
Covey, R. Alan
2006 *How the Incas Built Their Heartland: State Formation and the Innovation of Imperial Strategies in the Sacred Valley, Peru.* University of Michigan Press, Ann Arbor.
Cummins, Thomas B. F.
2008 The Felicitous Legacy of the Lanzón. In *Chavín: Art, Architecture, and Culture*, edited by William J. Conklin and Jeffrey Quilter, pp. 279–304. Monograph 61. Cotsen Institute of Archaeology, University of California, Los Angeles.
Cutright, Robyn E.
2009 *Between the Kitchen and the State: Domestic Practice and Chimú Expansion in the Jequetepeque Valley, Peru.* Unpublished PhD dissertation, Department of Anthropology, University of Pittsburgh.
2010 Food, Family, and Empire: Relating Political and Domestic Change in the Jequetepeque Hinterland. In *Comparative Perspectives on the Archaeology of Coastal South America*, edited by Robyn E. Cutright, Enrique López-Hurtado, and Alexander J. Martín, pp. 27–44. Center for Comparative Archaeology, University of Pittsburgh, Pittsburgh.
Cutright, Robyn, and Carlos Osores Mendives
2021 A Tale of Two Cities?: Neighborhood Identity and Integration at Ventanillas. In *Sociopolitical Integration in Prehispanic Neighborhoods*, edited by Gabriela Cervantes and John Walden. Center for Comparative Archaeology, University of Pittsburgh, Pittsburgh, in press. Ms. 2019.

Davenport, William
1960 Jamaican Fishing: A Game Theory Analysis. *Yale University Publications in Anthropology* 59:3–11.
DeMarrais, Elizabeth, Luis Jaime Castillo, and Timothy Earle
1996 Ideology, Materialization, and Power Strategies. *Current Anthropology* 37(1):15–31.
Despres, Leo A.
1975 Toward a Theory of Ethnic Phenomena. In *Ethnicity and Resource Competition in Plural Societies*, edited by Leo A. Despres, pp. 187–207. Mouton, The Hague.
Dillehay, Tom D.
1976 Competition and Cooperation in a Prehispanic Multi-Ethnic System in the Central Andes. Unpublished PhD dissertation, Department of Anthropology, University of Texas, Austin.
1977 Tawantinsuyu Integration of the Chillon Valley, Peru: A Case of Inca Geo-Political Mastery. *Journal of Field Archaeology* 4(4):397–405.
2001 Town and Country in Late Moche Times: A View from Two Northern Valleys. *Studies in the History of Art* 63:258–283.
Dillehay, Tom D., Alan L. Kolata, and Edward R. Swenson
2009 *Paisajes culturales en el valle del Jequetepeque: Los yacimientos arqueológicos.* SIAN, Trujillo, Peru.
Dillehay, Tom D., and Patricia J. Netherly
1983 Exploring the Upper Zaña Valley in Peru. *Archaeology* 36(4):22–30.
Dillehay, Tom D., Patricia J. Netherly, and Jack Rossen
1989 Middle Preceramic Public and Residential Sites on the Forested Slope of the Western Andes, Northern Peru. *American Antiquity* 54(4):733–759.
Disselhoff, Hans D.
1958 Cajamarca-Keramik von der Pampa von San José de Moro (Prov. Pacasmayo). *Baessler-Archiv* 6:181–193.
Donnan, Christopher B.
1971 Ancient Peruvian Potters' Marks and Their Interpretation through Ethnographic Analogy. *American Antiquity* 36(4):460–466.
1986a The City Walls at Pacatnamu. In *The Pacatnamu Papers*, edited by Christopher B. Donnan and Guillermo A. Cock, pp. 47–62. Vol. 1. Museum of Cultural History, University of California, Los Angeles.
1986b The Huaca 1 Complex. In *The Pacatnamu Papers*, edited by Christopher B. Donnan and Guillermo A. Cock, pp. 63–84. Vol. 1. Museum of Cultural History, University of California, Los Angeles.
1986c Introduction. In *The Pacatnamu Papers*, edited by Christopher B. Donnan and Guillermo A. Cock, pp. 19–26. Vol. 1. Museum of Cultural History, University of California, Los Angeles.
1997 A Chimu-Inka Ceramic-Manufacturing Center from the North Coast of Peru. *Latin American Antiquity* 8(1):30–54.
2012 *Chotuna and Chornancap: Excavating an Ancient Peruvian Legend.* Cotsen Institute of Archaeology, University of California, Los Angeles.

Donnan, Christopher B., and Carol J. Mackey
1978 *Ancient Burial Patterns of the Moche Valley, Peru.* University of Texas Press, Austin.
Doyle, Mary Eileen
1988 *The Ancestor Cult and Burial Ritual in Seventeenth and Eighteenth Century Central Peru.* PhD dissertation, University of California, Los Angeles. University Microfilms, Ann Arbor.
Driessen, Henk
1992 *On the Spanish-Moroccan Frontier: A Study in Ritual, Power, and Ethnicity.* St. Martin's Press, New York.
Durkheim, Emile
1893 *De la division du travail social: Étude sur l'organisation des sociétés supérieures.* Félix Alcan, Paris.
1912 *Les formes élémentaire de la vie religieuse: Le système totémique en Australie.* Félix Alcan, Paris.
Durston, Alan
2007 Notes on the Authorship of the Huarochirí Manuscript. *Colonial Latin American Review* 16(2):227–241.
Eling, Herbert H., Jr.
1987 *The Role of Irrigation Networks in Emerging Societal Complexity during Late Prehispanic Times, Jequetepeque, North Coast, Peru.* PhD dissertation, University of Texas, Austin. University Microfilms, Ann Arbor.
Emberling, Geoff
1997 Ethnicity in Complex Societies: Archaeological Perspectives. *Journal of Archaeological Research* 5(4):295–344.
Eriksen, Thomas Hylland
2015 *Fredrik Barth: An Intellectual Biography.* Pluto, London.
Espinoza Soriano, Waldemar
1967 El primer informe etnológico sobre Cajamarca: Año de 1540. *Revista Peruana de Historia* 11–12:1–37.
1977 La poliginia señorial en el reino de Caxamarca: Siglos XV y XVI. *Revista del Museo Nacional* 43:399–466.
Feldman, Robert A.
1985 Preceramic Corporate Architecture: Evidence for the Development of Non-Egalitarian Social Systems in Peru. In *Early Ceremonial Architecture in the Andes,* edited by Christopher B. Donnan, pp. 71–92. Dumbarton Oaks, Washington, DC.
Flannery, Kent V., Joyce Marcus, and Robert G. Reynolds
1989 *The Flocks of the Wamani: A Study of Llama Herders on the Punas of Ayacucho, Peru.* Academic Press, San Diego.
Fried, Morton H.
1966 On the Concept of "Tribe" and Tribal Society. *Transactions of the New York Academy of Sciences,* Series 2, 28(4):527–540.
1975 *The Notion of Tribe.* Cummings, Menlo Park, California.

Garcilaso de la Vega, El Inca
1966 [1609] *Royal Commentaries of the Incas and General History of Peru.* Translated by Harold V. Livermore. Part 1. University of Texas Press, Austin.
Gathercole, Peter
2009 Childe, Marxism, and Knowledge. *European Journal of Archaeology* 12(1–3): 181–191.
Gillin, John P.
1947 *Moche: A Peruvian Coastal Community.* Publication No. 3. Institute of Social Anthropology, Smithsonian Institution, Washington, DC.
Glowacki, Mary, and Michael Malpass
2003 Water, Huacas, and Ancestor Worship: Traces of a Sacred Wari Landscape. *Latin American Antiquity* 14(4):431–448.
Goldstein, Paul S.
2005 *Andean Diaspora: The Tiwanaku Colonies and the Origins of South American Empire.* University Press of Florida, Gainesville.
2015 Multiethnicity, Pluralism, and Migration in the South Central Andes: An Alternate Path to State Expansion. *Proceedings of the National Academy of Sciences* 112(30):9202–9209.
González Holguín, Diego
1952 [1608] *Vocabulario de la lengua general de todo el Pirú llamada lengua Quichua o del Inca.* Edición del Instituto de Historia, Universidad Nacional Mayor de San Marcos, Lima.
Grobman, Alexander, Wilfredo Salhuana, and Ricardo Sevilla
1961 *Races of Maize in Peru: Their Origins, Evolution and Classification.* National Academy of Sciences-National Research Council, Washington, DC.
Guaman Poma de Ayala, Felipe
1993 [1615] *Nueva corónica y buen gobierno.* Translated by Jan Szemiñski. Vol. 1. Fondo de Cultura Económica, Mexico City.
Harris, Marvin
1968 *The Rise of Anthropological Theory: A History of Theories of Culture.* Crowell, New York.
Harlow, Harry F.
1949 The Formation of Learning Sets. *Psychological Review* 56(1):51–65.
Hart, Elizabeth A.
1983 Prehispanic Political Organization of the Peruvian North Coast. Unpublished PhD dissertation, Department of Anthropology, University of Michigan, Ann Arbor.
Hodder, Ian
1977 The Distribution of Material Culture Items in the Baringo District, Western Kenya. *Man* 12(2):239–269.
1982 *Symbols in Action: Ethnoarchaeological Studies of Material Culture.* Cambridge University Press, Cambridge.
Holmberg, Allan R.
1950 Viru: Remnant of an Exalted People. In *Patterns for Modern Living.* Divison 3: Cultural Patterns, pp. 367–416. The Delphian Society, Chicago.

Hornberger, Esteban, and Nancy H. Hornberger
2008 *Diccionario trilingüe quechua de Cusco: Qhiswa, English, Castellano.* Centro Bartolomé de Las Casas, Cusco.
Huarochirí Manuscript
1991 [ca. 1608] *The Huarochirí Manuscript: A Testament of Ancient and Colonial Andean Religion.* Translated by Frank Salomon and George L. Urioste. University of Texas Press, Austin.
Hüsken, Ute (editor)
2007 *When Rituals Go Wrong: Mistakes, Failure and the Dynamics of Ritual.* Brill, Leiden.
Hymes, Dell H. (editor)
1968 *Essays on the Problem of Tribe.* University of Washington Press, Seattle.
Irvine, Judith T., and Susan Gal
2000 Language Ideology and Linguistic Differentiation. In *Regimes of Language: Ideologies, Polities, and Identities,* edited by Paul V. Kroskrity, pp. 35–83. School of American Research Press, Santa Fe, New Mexico.
Isbell, Billie Jean
1978 *To Defend Ourselves: Ecology and Ritual in an Andean Village.* Latin American Monographs No. 47. Institute of Latin American Studies, University of Texas, Austin.
Isbell, William H.
1977 *The Rural Foundation for Urbanism: Economic and Stylistic Interaction between Rural and Urban Communities in Eighth-Century Peru.* Illinois Studies in Anthropology No. 10. University of Illinois Press, Urbana.
2004 Mortuary Preferences: A Wari Culture Case Study from Middle Horizon Peru. *Latin American Antiquity* 15(1):3–32.
Jaeckel, Paul, and Alfredo Melly Cava
1987 Untitled summary of 1984 fieldwork. *Willay: Newsletter of the Andean Anthropological Research Group* 25:7–9.
Janusek, John W.
2009 Residence and Ritual in Tiwanaku: Hierarchy, Specialization, Ethnicity, and Ceremony. In *Domestic Life in Prehispanic Capitals: A Study of Specialization, Hierarchy, and Ethnicity,* edited by Linda R. Manzanilla and Claude Chapdelaine, pp. 159–179. Memoirs No. 46. Museum of Anthropology, University of Michigan, Ann Arbor.
Jones, Siân
1997 *The Archaeology of Ethnicity: Constructing Identities in the Past and Present.* Routledge, London.
Joralemon, Donald, and Douglas Sharon
1993 *Sorcery and Shamanism: Curanderos and Clients in Northern Peru.* University of Utah Press, Salt Lake City.
Julien, Catherine J.
1982 Inka Decimal Administration in the Lake Titicaca Region. In *The Inca and*

Aztec States, 1400–1800: Anthropology and History, edited by George A. Collier, Renato I. Rosaldo, and John D. Wirth, pp. 119–151. Academic Press, New York.

Julien, Daniel G.

1988 Ancient Cuismancu: Settlement and Cultural Dynamics in the Cajamarca Region of the North Highlands of Peru, 200 B.C.–A.D. 1532. PhD dissertation, University of Texas, Austin. University Microfilms, Ann Arbor.

1993 Late Pre-Inkaic Ethnic Groups in Highland Peru: An Archaeological-Ethnohistorical Model of the Political Geography of the Cajamarca Region. *Latin American Antiquity* 4(3):246–273.

Keane, Webb

1997 *Signs of Recognition: Powers and Hazards of Representation in an Indonesian Society*. University of California Press, Berkeley.

Keatinge, Richard W.

1980 Archaeology and Development: The Tembladera Sites of the Peruvian North Coast. *Journal of Field Archaeology* 7(4):467–477.

1982 The Chimú Empire in a Regional Perspective: Cultural Antecedents and Continuities. In *Chan Chan: Andean Desert City*, edited by Michael E. Moseley and Kent C. Day, pp. 197–224. University of New Mexico Press, Albuquerque.

Kelly, Robert L.

2011 Lewis R. Binford (1931–2011). *Science* 332(6032):928.

Kolata, Alan L.

1982 Chronology and Settlement Growth at Chan Chan. In *Chan Chan: Andean Desert City*, edited by Michael E. Moseley and Kent C. Day, pp. 67–85. University of New Mexico Press, Albuquerque.

1990 The Urban Concept of Chan Chan. In *The Northern Dynasties: Kingship and Statecraft in Chimor*, edited by Michael E. Moseley and Alana Cordy-Collins, pp. 107–144. Dumbarton Oaks Research Library and Collection, Washington, DC.

Kolata, Alan L. (editor)

2003a *Tiwanaku and Its Hinterland: Archaeology and Paleoecology of an Andean Civilization*. Vol. 2: *Urban and Rural Archaeology*. Smithsonian Institution Press, Washington, DC.

2003b Tiwanaku Ceremonial Architecture and Urban Organization. In *Tiwanaku and Its Hinterland: Archaeology and Paleoecology of an Andean Civilization. Vol. 2: Urban and Rural Archaeology*, edited by Alan Kolata, pp. 30–92. Smithsonian Institution Press, Washington, DC.

Kosok, Paul

1965 *Life, Land and Water in Ancient Peru*. Long Island University Press, New York.

Kossinna, Gustaf

1881 *Über die ältesten hochfränkischen Sprachdenkmäler*. K. J. Trübner, Strassburg.

1911 *Die Herkunft der Germanen: Zur Methode der Siedlungsarchäologie*. Würzburg, C. Kabitzsch.

1926 *Ursprung und Verbreitung der Germanen in vorund frühgeschichtlicher Zeit*. Germanenverlag, Berlin.

Kroeber, Alfred L.

1925 The Uhle Pottery Collection from Moche. *University of California Publications in American Archaeology and Ethnology* 21(5):191–234.

1944 *Peruvian Archaeology in 1942*. Viking Fund Publications in Anthropology No. 4. Wenner-Gren Foundation for Anthropological Research, New York.

1948 *Anthropology: Culture Patterns and Processes*. Harcourt, Brace & World, New York.

Larco Hoyle, Rafael

1948 *Cronología arqueológica del norte del Perú*. Sociedad Geográfica Americana, Buenos Aires.

Lau, George F.

2004 Object of Contention: An Examination of Recuay-Moche Combat Imagery. *Cambridge Archaeological Journal* 14(2):163–184.

2006 Northern Exposures: Recuay-Cajamarca Boundaries and Interaction. In *Andean Archaeology III: North and South*, edited by William H. Isbell and Helaine Silverman, pp. 143–170. Springer, New York.

2010 *Ancient Community and Economy at Chinchawas (Ancash, Peru)*. Yale University Press, New Haven.

2013 *Ancient Alterity in the Andes: A Recognition of Others*. Routledge, London.

Leach, Edmund R.

1954 *Political Systems of Highland Burma: A Study of Kachin Social Structure*. Harvard University Press, Cambridge, Massachusetts.

1962 On Certain Unconsidered Aspects of Double Descent Systems. *Man* 62: 130–134.

1973 Concluding Address. In *The Explanation of Culture Change: Models in Prehistory*, edited by Colin Renfrew, pp. 761–771. University of Pittsburgh Press, Pittsburgh.

1990 Aryan Invasions over Four Millennia. In *Culture through Time: Anthropological Approaches*, edited by Emiko Ohnuki-Tierney, pp. 227–245. Stanford University Press, Stanford.

Mackey, Carol J.

1987 Chimu Administration in the Provinces. In *The Origins and Development of the Andean State*, edited by Jonathan Haas, Shelia Pozorski, and Thomas Pozorski, pp. 121–129. Cambridge University Press, Cambridge.

2006 Elite Residences at Farfán: A Comparison of the Chimú and Inka Occupations. In *Palaces and Power in the Americas: From Peru to the Northwest Coast*, edited by Jessica Joyce Christie and Patricia Joan Sarro, pp. 313–352. University of Texas Press, Austin.

2009 Chimú Statecraft in the Provinces. In *Andean Civilization: A Tribute to Michael E. Moseley*, edited by Joyce Marcus and Patrick Ryan Williams, pp. 325–349. Monograph 63. Cotsen Institute of Archaeology, University of California, Los Angeles.

2011 The Persistence of Lambayeque Ethnic Identity: The Perspective from the Jequetepeque Valley, Peru. In *From State to Empire in the Prehistoric Jequetepeque Val-*

ley, Peru, edited by Colleen M. Zori and Ilana Johnson, pp. 149–168. Archaeopress, Oxford.

Mannheim, Bruce
1998 A Nation Surrounded. In *Native Traditions in the Postconquest World*, edited by Elizabeth Hill Boone and Tom Cummins, pp. 383–420. Dumbarton Oaks Research Library and Collection, Washington, DC.

Mannheim, Bruce, and Dennis Tedlock (editors)
1995 *The Dialogic Emergence of Culture*. University of Illinois Press, Urbana.

Manzanilla, Linda R.
2009 Corporate Life in Apartment and Barrio Compounds at Teotihuacan, Central Mexico: Craft Specialization, Hierarchy, and Ethnicity. In *Domestic Life in Prehispanic Capitals: A Study of Specialization, Hierarchy, and Ethnicity*, edited by Linda R. Manzanilla and Claude Chapdelaine, pp. 21–42. Memoirs No. 46. Museum of Anthropology, University of Michigan, Ann Arbor.

Marcus, Joyce
1987 Prehistoric Fishermen in the Kingdom of Huarco. *American Scientist* 75(4): 393–401.
1998 The Peaks and Valleys of Ancient States: An Extension of the Dynamic Model. In *Archaic States*, edited by Gary M. Feinman and Joyce Marcus, pp. 59–94. School of American Research Press, Santa Fe, New Mexico.
2000 Toward an Archaeology of Communities. In *The Archaeology of Communities: A New World Perspective*, edited by Jason Yaeger and Marcello A. Canuto, pp. 231–242. Routledge, London.
2007 Rethinking Ritual. In *The Archaeology of Ritual*, edited by Evangelos Kyriakidis, pp. 43–76. Cotsen Institute of Archaeology, University of California, Los Angeles.
2008a The Archaeological Evidence for Social Evolution. *Annual Review of Anthropology* 37:251–266.
2008b *Excavations at Cerro Azul, Peru: The Architecture and Pottery*. Monograph 62. Cotsen Institute of Archaeology, University of California, Los Angeles.
2009 Understanding Houses, Compounds, and Neighborhoods. In *Domestic Life in Prehispanic Capitals: A Study of Specialization, Hierarchy, and Ethnicity*, edited by Linda R. Manzanilla and Claude Chapdelaine, pp. 257–266. Memoirs No. 46. Museum of Anthropology, University of Michigan, Ann Arbor.

Marcus, Joyce, and Kent V. Flannery
1996 *Zapotec Civilization: How Urban Society Evolved in Mexico's Oaxaca Valley*. Thames and Hudson, New York.

Marcus, Joyce, and Jorge E. Silva
1988 The Chillón Valley "Coca Lands": Archaeological Background and Ecological Context. In *Conflicts Over Coca Fields in XVIth-Century Perú*, pp. 1–32. Memoirs No. 21. Museum of Anthropology, University of Michigan, Ann Arbor.

Matsumoto, Ryozo
1982 Classification of Pottery. In *Excavations at Huacaloma in the Cajamarca Valley,*

Peru, 1979, edited by Kazuo Terada and Yoshio Onuki, pp. 93–117. Report 2 of the Japanese Scientific Expedition to Nuclear America. University of Tokyo Press, Tokyo.

Matsumoto, Ryozo, and Tsuyoshi Ushino

1982 Clay, Stone, Metal, Bone and Shell Artifacts. In *Excavations at Huacaloma in the Cajamarca Valley, Peru, 1979*, edited by Kazuo Terada and Yoshio Onuki, pp. 181–220. Report 2 of the Japanese Scientific Expedition to Nuclear America. University of Tokyo Press, Tokyo.

Mayer, Enrique

1977 Beyond the Nuclear Family. In *Andean Kinship and Marriage*, edited by Ralph Bolton and Enrique Mayer, pp. 60–80. American Anthropological Association, Washington, DC.

2002 *The Articulated Peasant: Household Economies in the Andes*. Westview Press, Boulder, Colorado.

McClelland, Donald H.

1986 Brick Seriation at Pacatnamu. In *The Pacatnamu Papers*, edited by Christopher B. Donnan and Guillermo A. Cock, pp. 27–46. Vol. 1. Museum of Cultural History, University of California, Los Angeles.

McClelland, Donna

2008 *Ulluchu*: An Elusive Fruit. In *The Art and Archaeology of the Moche: An Ancient Andean Society of the Peruvian North Coast*, edited by Steve Bourget and Kimberly L. Jones, pp. 43–65. University of Texas Press, Austin.

McClelland, Donna, Donald H. McClelland, and Christopher B. Donnan

2007 *Moche Fineline Painting from San José de Moro*. Cotsen Institute of Archaeology, University of California, Los Angeles.

McCown, Theodore D.

1945 *Pre-Incaic Huamachuco: Survey and Excavations in the Region of Huamachuco and Cajabamba*. University of California Publications in American Archaeology and Ethnology 39(4). University of California Press, Berkeley and Los Angeles.

McEwan, Gordon F.

2005 Excavations at Pikillacta. In *Pikillacta: The Wari Empire in Cuzco*, edited by Gordon F. McEwan, pp. 29–62. University of Iowa Press, Iowa City.

Means, Philip A.

1964 *Ancient Civilizations of the Andes*. Gordian Press, New York.

Medina, Felipe de

1904 [1650] Relación del licenciado Felipe de Medina, Visitador General de las Idolatrías del Arzobispado de Lima, inviada al ilustrísimo y reverendísimo Señor Arzobispo della, en que le da cuenta de las que se han descubierto en el pueblo de Huacho, donde ha comenzado á visitar desde 19 de febrero hasta 23 de marzo de 1650. In *La Imprenta en Lima (1584–1824), Tomo I (1584–1650)*, edited by José Toribio Medina, pp. 215–221. Fondo Editorial José Toribio Medina, Santiago de Chile.

Menzel, Dorothy

1977 *The Archaeology of Ancient Peru and the Work of Max Uhle*. R. H. Lowie Museum of Anthropology University of California, Berkeley.

Miller, George R.
1979 *An Introduction to the Ethnoarchaeology of the Andean Camelids.* PhD dissertation, Department of Anthropology, University of California, Berkeley. University Microfilms, Ann Arbor.
Molina, Cristóbal de
1989 [1575] Relación de las fábulas i ritos de los ingas hecha por Cristóbal de Molina, cura de la parroquia de Nestra Señora de los Remedios, de el Hospital de los naturales de la ciudad de el Cuzco, dirigida al reverendísimo señor Obispo don Sebastián de el Artaum, del consejo de su magestad. In *Fábulos y mitos de los incas*, edited by Henrique Urbano and Pierre Duviols, pp. 47–134. Historia 16, Madrid.
Montenegro, Jorge
1993 Estilo Cajamarca Costeño: Una aproximación. In *IX Congreso peruano del hombre y la cultura andina*, edited by Segundo Arréstegui, pp. 137–144. Vol. 1. Universidad Nacional de Cajamarca, Cajamarca.
1997 Coastal Cajamarca Pottery from the North Coast of Peru: Style, Technology, and Function. Unpublished master's thesis, Department of Anthropology, Southern Illinois University, Carbondale.
Moore, Jerry D.
1996a *Architecture and Power in the Ancient Andes: The Archaeology of Public Buildings.* Cambridge University Press, Cambridge.
1996b The Archaeology of Plazas and the Proxemics of Ritual: Three Andean Traditions. *American Anthropologist* 98(4):789–802.
Moore, Jerry D., and Carol J. Mackey
2008 The Chimú Empire. In *The Handbook of South American Archaeology*, edited by Helaine Silverman and William H. Isbell, pp. 783–807. Springer, New York.
Morris, Craig, and Donald E. Thompson
1985 *Huánuco Pampa: An Inca City and Its Hinterland.* Thames and Hudson, London.
Moseley, Michael E.
1982 Introduction: Human Exploitation and Organization on the North Andean Coast. In *Chan Chan: Andean Desert City*, edited by Michael E. Moseley and Kent C. Day, pp. 1–24. University of New Mexico Press, Albuquerque.
2001 *The Incas and Their Ancestors: The Archaeology of Peru.* 2nd ed. Thames and Hudson, London.
Moseley, Michael E., Christopher B. Donnan, and David K. Keefer
2008 Convergent Catastrophe and the Demise of Dos Cabezas: Environmental Change and Regime Change in Ancient Peru. In *The Art and Archaeology of the Moche: An Ancient Andean Society of the Peruvian North Coast*, edited by Steve Bourget and Kimberly L. Jones, pp. 81–91. University of Texas Press, Austin.
Moseley, Michael E., Donna J. Nash, Patrick Ryan Williams, Susan D. deFrance, Ana Miranda, and Mario Ruales
2005 Burning Down the Brewery: Establishing and Evacuating an Ancient Imperial Colony at Cerro Baúl, Peru. *Proceedings of the National Academy of Sciences of the United States of America* 102(48):17264–17271.

Muelle, Jorge C., and Camilo Blas
1938 Muestrario de arte precolombino. I-Cerámica. *Revista del Museo Nacional* 7(2):163–280.

Murra, John V.
1972 El "control vertical" de un máximo de pisos ecológicos en la economía de las sociedades andinas. In *Visita de la provincia de León de Huánuco en 1562*, edited by John V. Murra, pp. 427–476. Vol. 2. Universidad Nacional Hermilio Valdizán, Huánuco, Peru.
1980 *The Economic Organization of the Inka State*. Research in Economic Anthropology, Supplement 1. JAI Press, Greenwich, Connecticut.

Naroll, Raoul
1964 On Ethnic Unit Classification. *Current Anthropology* 5:283–312.

Narváez, Alfredo
1995 The Pyramids of Túcume: The Monumental Sector. In *Pyramids of Túcume: The Quest for Peru's Forgotten City*, edited by Thor Heyerdahl, Daniel H. Sandweiss, and Alfredo Narváez, pp. 79–130. Thames and Hudson, New York.

Nash, Donna J., and Patrick Ryan Williams
2009 Wari Political Organization: The Southern Periphery. In *Andean Civilization: A Tribute to Michael E. Moseley*, edited by Joyce Marcus and Patrick Ryan Williams, pp. 257–276. Monograph 63. Cotsen Institute of Archaeology, University of California, Los Angeles.

Nelson, Andrew J., Christine S. Nelson, Luis Jaime Castillo, and Carol J. Mackey
2000 Osteobiografía de una hilandera precolombina: La mujer detrás de la máscara. *Íconos* 4(2):30–43.

Netherly, Patricia J.
1988 From Event to Process: The Recovery of Late Andean Organizational Structure by Means of Spanish Colonial Written Records. In *Peruvian Prehistory: An Overview of Pre-Inca and Inca Society*, edited by Richard W. Keatinge, pp. 257–275. University of Cambridge Press, Cambridge.

O'Shea, John M.
1996 *Villagers of the Maros: A Portrait of an Early Bronze Age Society*. Plenum Press, New York.

ONERN (Oficina Nacional de Evaluación de Recursos Naturales)
1975 *Inventario, evaluación y uso racional de los recursos naturales de la zona sur del departamento de Cajamarca*. Vol. 1. Oficina Nacional de Evaluación de Recursos Naturales, Lima.
1988 *Plan de ordenamiento ambiental de la cuenca del río Jequetepeque para la protección del reservorio Gallito Ciego y del valle agícola*. Oficina Nacional de Evaluación de Recursos Naturales, Lima.

Onuki, Yoshio
1985 The Yunga Zone in the Prehistory of the Central Andes: Vertical and Horizontal Dimensions in Andean Ecological and Cultural Processes. In *Andean Ecology and Civilization: An Interdisciplinary Perspective on Andean Ecological Complemen-*

tarity, edited by Shozo Masuda, Izumi Shimada, and Craig Morris, pp. 339–356. University of Tokyo Press, Tokyo.

Onuki, Yoshio (editor)
1995 *Kuntur Wasi y Cerro Blanco: Dos sitios del formativo en el norte del Perú.* Hokusen-sha, Tokyo.

Ortiz, Alfonso
1969 *The Tewa World: Space, Time, Being, and Becoming in a Pueblo Society.* University of Chicago Press, Chicago.

Owen, Bruce D.
2005 Distant Colonies and Explosive Collapse: The Two Stages of the Tiwanaku Diaspora in the Osmore Drainage. *Latin American Antiquity* 16(1):45–80.

Parsons, Jeffrey R.
2009 Reflections on My Life in Archaeology. *Ancient Mesoamerica* 20(1):3–13.

Parsons, Jeffrey R., Charles M. Hastings, and Matos M. Ramiro
2000 *Prehispanic Settlement Patterns in the Upper Mantaro and Tarma Drainages, Junín, Peru.* Memoirs No. 4, Vol. 1, The Tarama-Chinchaycocha Region, Part 1. Museum of Anthropology, University of Michigan, Ann Arbor.

Parsons, Mary Hrones
1972 Spindle Whorls from the Teotihuacán Valley, Mexico. In *Miscellaneous Studies in Mexican Prehistory.* Anthropological Papers No. 45. Museum of Anthropology, University of Michigan, Ann Arbor.
1975 The Distribution of Late Postclassic Spindle Whorls in the Valley of Mexico. *American Antiquity* 40(2):207–215.

Pärssinen, Martti
2003 *Tawantinsuyu: El estado inca y su organización política.* Instituto Francés de Estudios Andinos, Lima.

Paulsen, Allison C.
1974 The Thorny Oyster and the Voice of God: *Spondylus* and *Strombus* in Andean Prehistory. *American Antiquity* 39(4):597–607.

Peace, William J.
2007 *Leslie A. White: Evolution and Revolution in Anthropology.* University of Nebraska Press, Lincoln.

Piggott, Stuart
1970 *Ancient Europe: From the Beginnings of Agriculture to Classical Antiquity.* Aldine, Chicago.

Pimentel, Victor
1986 *Felszeichnungen im mittleren und unteren Jequetepeque-Tal, Nord-Peru.* C. H. Beck, Munich.

Pleck, Elizabeth H.
2000 *Celebrating the Family: Ethnicity, Consumer Culture, and Family Rituals.* Harvard University Press, Cambridge, Massachusetts.

Plowman, Timothy
1979 Botanical Perspectives on Coca. *Journal of Psychedelic Drugs* 11(1–2):103–117.

Polo de Ondegardo, Juan
1999 [1571] Del linaje de los yngas y como conquistaron. In *Polo de Ondegardo: Un cronista vallisoletano en el Perú*, edited by Laura González Pujana, pp. 344–367. Instituto de Estudios de Iberoamérica y Portugal, Universidad de Valladolid, Valladolid.

Prieto Burmester, O. Gabriel
2010 Approximating Lambayeque Political Configurations: A Perspective from the Site of San José de Moro, Jequetepeque Valley. In *Comparative Perspectives on the Archaeology of Coastal South America*, edited by Robyn E. Cutright, Enrique López-Hurtado, and Alexander J. Martín, pp. 231–246. Center for Comparative Archaeology, University of Pittsburgh, Pittsburgh.

Proulx, Donald A.
1982 Territoriality in the Early Intermediate Period. *Ñawpa Pacha* 20:83–96.

Ramírez, Susan E.
1996 *The World Upside Down: Cross-Cultural Contact and Conflict in Sixteenth-Century Peru.* Stanford University Press, Stanford.
1998 Rich Man, Poor Man, Beggar Man, or Chief: Material Wealth as a Basis of Power in Sixteenth-Century Peru. In *Dead Giveaways: Indigenous Testaments of Colonial Mesoamerica and the Andes*, edited by Susan Kellogg and Matthew Restall, pp. 215–248. University of Utah Press, Salt Lake City.

Rappaport, Roy A.
1999 *Ritual and Religion in the Making of Humanity.* Cambridge University Press, Cambridge.

Ravines, Rogger
1982 *Arqueología del valle medio del Jequetepeque.* Instituto Nacional de Cultura, Lima.

Reichlen, Henry, and Paule Reichlen
1949 Recherches archéologiques dans les Andes de Cajamarca: Premier rapport de la Mission ethnologique française au Pérou septentrional. *Journal de la Société des Américanistes* 38:137–174.

Reindel, Markus
1993 *Monumentale Lehmarchitektur an der Nordküste Perus: Eine Repräsentative Untersuchung Nach-Formativer Grossbauten vom Lambayeque-Gebiet bis zum Virú-Tal.* Holos, Bonn.

Remy, Pilar
1992 El documento. In *Las visitas a Cajamarca 1571–72/1578*, edited by María Rostworowski de Diez Canseco and Pilar Remy, pp. 37–108. Vol. 1. Instituto de Estudios Peruanos, Lima.

Renfrew, Colin
1986 Introduction: Peer Polity Interaction and Socio-Political Change. In *Peer Polity Interaction and Socio-Political Change*, edited by Colin Renfrew and John F. Cherry, pp. 1–18. Cambridge University Press, Cambridge.

Renfrew, Colin, and Paul Bahn
1996 *Archaeology: Theories, Methods, and Practice.* Thames and Hudson, London.

Reycraft, Richard Martin (editor)
2005 *Us and Them: Archaeology and Ethnicity in the Andes.* Cotsen Institute of Archaeology, University of California, Los Angeles.

Rick, John W.
1980 *Prehistoric Hunters of the High Andes.* Academic Press, New York.

Rosas, Hermilio, and Ruth Shady
1970 *Pacopampa: Un centro formativo en la sierra nor-peruana.* Seminario de Historia Rural Andina, Universidad Nacional Mayor de San Marcos, Lima.

Rosas Rintel, Marco
2007 Nuevas perspectivas acerca del colapso Moche en el Bajo Jequetepeque: Resultados preliminares de la segunda campaña de investigación del proyecto arqueológico Cerro Chepén. *Bulletin de l'Institut Français d'Études Andines* 36(2):221–240.

Rostworowski de Diez Canseco, María
1973 Plantaciones prehispánicas de coca en la vertiente del Pacífico. *Revista del Museo Nacional* 39:193–224.
1977 *Etnía y sociedad: Costa peruana prehispánica.* Instituto de Estudios Peruanos, Lima.
1978 *Señoríos indígenas de Lima y Canta.* Instituto de Estudios Peruanos, Lima.
1988 *Conflicts Over Coca Fields in XVIth-Century Perú.* Memoirs No. 21. Museum of Anthropology, University of Michigan, Ann Arbor.

Rostworowski de Diez Canseco, María, and Pilar Remy (editors)
1992 *Las visitas a Cajamarca 1571–72/1578: Documentos.* 2 vols. Instituto de Estudios Peruanos, Lima.

Rowe, John H.
1948 The Kingdom of Chimor. *Acta Americana* 6:26–59.

Ruiz Estrada, Arturo
2006 Exploraciones arqueológicas en la huaca Choque Ispana, valle de Huaura. *Investigaciones sociales: Revista del Instituto de Investigaciones Histórico Sociales* 10(16):151–169.

Sachún, Jorge
1986 *Patrones de asentamiento en el proceso cultural prehispánico del valle de Cajamarca (primera aproximación).* Materiales para la Arqueología de Cajamarca No. 3. Editorial Sudamérica, Trujillo.

Sahlins, Marshall
1985 *Islands of History.* University of Chicago Press, Chicago.

Sallnow, Michael J.
1987 *Pilgrims of the Andes: Regional Cults in Cusco.* Smithsonian Institution Press, Washington, DC.

Salomon, Frank
1991 Introductory Essay: The Huarochirí Manuscript. In *The Huarochirí Manuscript: A Testament of Ancient and Colonial Andean Religion*, pp. 1–38. University of Texas Press, Austin.

Santoro, Calogero M., Tom D. Dillehay, Jorge Hidalgo, Daniela Valenzuela R., Álvaro L. Romero G., Francisco Rothhammer, and Vivien G. Standen

2010 Revisita al tercer caso de verticalidad de John Murra en las costas de los andes centrales y centro sur. *Chungará* 42(1):325–340.

Sapir, Edward

1994 *The Psychology of Culture: A Course of Lectures.* Reconstructed and edited by Judith T. Irvine. Mouton de Gruyter, Berlin.

Sapp, William D.

2002 *The Impact of Imperial Conquest at the Palace of a Local Lord in the Jequetepeque Valley, Northern Perú.* PhD dissertation, University of California, Los Angeles. University Microfilms, Ann Arbor.

2011 Lambayeque Norte and Lambayeque Sur: Evidence for the Development of an Indigenous Lambayeque Polity in the Jequetepeque Valley. In *From State to Empire in the Prehistoric Jequetepeque Valley, Peru*, edited by Colleen M. Zori and Ilana Johnson, pp. 93–104. Archaeopress, Oxford.

Sarmiento de Gamboa, Pedro

2007 [1572] *The History of the Incas.* Translated by Brian S. Bauer and Vania Smith. University of Texas Press, Austin.

Scott, James C.

2009 *The Art of Not Being Governed: An Anarchist History of Upland Southeast Asia.* Yale University Press, New Haven.

Service, Elman R.

1968 War and Our Contemporary Ancestors. In *War: The Anthropology of Armed Conflict and Aggression*, edited by Morton H. Fried, Marvin Harris, and Robert F. Murphy, pp. 160–167. Natural History Press, Garden City, New York.

1971 *Primitive Social Organization: An Evolutionary Perspective.* Random House, New York.

Seton-Watson, Hugh

1977 *Nations and States: An Enquiry into the Origins of Nations and the Politics of Nationalism.* Westview Press, Boulder, Colorado.

Sharon, Douglas

1978 *Wizard of the Four Winds: A Shaman's Story.* Free Press, New York.

Sherratt, Andrew

1989 V. Gordon Childe: Archaeology and Intellectual History. *Past & Present* 125:151–185.

Shimada, Izumi

1981 The Batan Grande-La Leche Archaeological Project: The First Two Years. *Journal of Field Archaeology* 8(4):405–446.

1982 Horizontal Archipelago and Coast-Highland Interaction in North Peru. In *El Hombre y su Ambiente en los Andes Centrales*, edited by Luìs Millones and Hiroyasu Tomoeda, pp. 137–210. Senri Ethnological Studies 10. National Museum of Ethnology, Osaka.

1990 Cultural Continuities and Discontinuities on the North Coast of Peru. In *The*

Northern Dynasties: Kingship and Statecraft in Chimor, edited by Michael E. Moseley and Alana Cordy-Collins, pp. 297–392. Dumbarton Oaks Research Library and Collection, Washington, DC.

1994 *Pampa Grande and the Mochica Culture*. University of Texas Press, Austin.

1997 Organizational Significance of Marked Bricks and Associated Construction Features on the North Peruvian Coast. In *Arquitectura y civilización en los Andes prehispánicos*, edited by Elisabeth Bonnier and Henning Bischof, pp. 62–89. Reiss Museum, Mannheim.

2000 The Late Prehispanic Coastal States. In *The Inca World: The Development of Pre-Columbian Peru, A.D. 1000–1534*, edited by Laura Laurencich Minelli, pp. 49–110. University of Oklahoma Press, Norman.

2010 Moche Sociopolitical Organization: Rethinking the Data, Approaches, and Models. In *New Perspectives on Moche Political Organization*, edited by Jeffrey Quilter and Luis Jaime Castillo, pp. 70–82. Dumbarton Oaks Research Library and Collection, Washington, DC.

Shimada, Izumi, Ken-ichi Shinoda, Julie Farnum, Robert Corruccini, and Hirokatsu Watanabe

2004 An Integrated Analysis of Pre-Hispanic Mortuary Practices: A Middle Sicán Case Study. *Current Anthropology* 45(3):369–402.

Smith, Michael E.

1979 A Further Criticism of the Type-Variety System: The Data Can't Be Used. *American Antiquity* 44(4):822–826.

2009 V. Gordon Childe and the Urban Revolution: An Historical Perspective on a Revolution in Urban Studies. *Town Planning Review* 80(1):3–29.

Spalding, Karen

1984 *Huarochirí: An Andean Society under Inca and Spanish Rule*. Stanford University Press, Stanford.

Spence, Michael W.

1992 Tlailotlacan, a Zapotec Enclave in Teotihuacan. In *Art, Ideology, and the City of Teotihuacan*, edited by Janet Catherine Berlo, pp. 59–88. Dumbarton Oaks Research Library and Collection, Washington, DC.

Spencer, Charles S.

1990 On the Tempo and Mode of State Formation: Neoevolutionism Reconsidered. *Journal of Anthropological Archaeology* 9(1):1–30.

Stanish, Charles

1989 Household Archeology: Testing Models of Zonal Complementarity in the South Central Andes. *American Anthropologist* 91(1):7–24.

1992 *Ancient Andean Political Economy*. University of Texas Press, Austin.

2017 *The Evolution of Human Co-Operation: Ritual and Social Complexity in Stateless Societies*. Cambridge University Press, Cambridge.

Stone, Tammy

2003 Social Identity and Ethnic Interaction in the Western Pueblos of the American Southwest. *Journal of Archaeological Method and Theory* 10(1):31–67.

Stovel, Emily M.
2013 Concepts of Ethnicity and Culture in Andean Archaeology. *Latin American Antiquity* 24(1):3–20.

Swenson, Edward R.
2004 *Ritual and Power in the Urban Hinterland: Religious Pluralism and Political Decentralization in Late Moche Jequetepeque, Peru.* PhD dissertation, University of Chicago. University Microfilms, Ann Arbor.
2006 Competitive Feasting, Religious Pluralism and Decentralized Power in the Late Moche Period. In *Andean Archaeology III: North and South*, edited by William H. Isbell and Helaine Silverman, pp. 112–142. Springer, New York.
2012 Warfare, Gender, and Sacrifice in Jequetepeque, Peru. *Latin American Antiquity* 23(2):167–193.

Swenson, Edward R., Jorge Y. Chiguala, and John P. Warner
2011 *Proyecto Arqueológico Jatanca-Huaca Colorada: Informe final de la temporada de investigación 2010.* Preliminary report submitted to the Instituto Nacional de Cultura, Lima. Copies available from the Instituto Nacional de Cultura, Cajamarca.

Tambiah, Stanley J.
2002 *Edmund Leach: An Anthropological Life.* Cambridge University Press, Cambridge.

Taylor, Gerald
2008 Introducción. In *Ritos y tradiciones de Huarochirí*, edited by Gerald Taylor, pp. 9–17. Instituto de Estudios Peruanos and Fondo Editorial Universidad Nacional Mayor de San Marcos, Lima.

Terada, Kazuo, and Ryozo Matsumoto
1985 Sobre la cronología de la tradición Cajamarca. In *Historia de Cajamarca. I. Arqueología*, edited by Fernando Silva Santisteban, Waldemar Espinoza Soriano, and Rogger Ravines, pp. 67–89. Instituto Nacional de Cultura, Cajamarca, Peru.

Terada, Kazuo, and Yoshio Onuki (editors)
1985 *The Formative Period in the Cajamarca Basin, Peru: Excavations at Huacaloma and Layzón, 1982.* University of Tokyo Press, Tokyo.

Toohey, Jason L.
2009 Community Organization, Militarism, and Ethnogenesis in the Late Prehistoric Northern Highlands of Peru. Unpublished PhD dissertation, Department of Anthropology, University of California, Santa Barbara.
2011 Formal and Stylistic Variation in the Ceramic Assemblage at the Late Intermediate Period Site of Yanaorco in the Cajamarca Highlands of Northern Peru. *Ñawpa Pacha* 31(2):171–200.

Topic, John R.
1982 Lower-Class Social and Economic Organization at Chan Chan. In *Chan Chan: Andean Desert City*, edited by Michael E. Moseley and Kent C. Day, pp. 145–175. University of New Mexico Press, Albuquerque.
1990 Craft Production in the Kingdom of Chimor. In *The Northern Dynasties: Kingship and Statecraft in Chimor*, edited by Michael E. Moseley and Alana Cordy-

Collins, pp. 145–176. Dumbarton Oaks Research Library and Collection, Washington, DC.

2009 Domestic Economy as Political Economy at Chan Chan, Perú. In *Domestic Life in Prehispanic Capitals: A Study of Specialization, Hierarchy, and Ethnicity*, edited by Linda R. Manzanilla and Claude Chapdelaine, pp. 221–242. Memoirs No. 46. Museum of Anthropology, University of Michigan, Ann Arbor.

Topic, John R., and Michael E. Moseley

1983 Chan Chan: A Case Study of Urban Change in Peru. *Ñawpa Pacha* 21:153–182.

Topic, Theresa Lange

1990 Territorial Expansion and the Kingdom of Chimor. In *The Northern Dynasties: Kingship and Statecraft in Chimor*, edited by Michael E. Moseley and Alana Cordy-Collins, pp. 177–194. Dumbarton Oaks Research Library and Collection, Washington, DC.

1991 The Middle Horizon in Northern Peru. In *Huari Administrative Structure: Prehistoric Monumental Architecture and State Government*, edited by William H. Isbell and Gordon F. McEwan, pp. 233–246. Dumbarton Oaks Research Library and Collection, Washington, DC.

1996 Cajamarca. In *The Dictionary of Art*, edited by Jane Turner, pp. 408–410. Vol. 5. Macmillan, London.

Townsend, Joan B.

1985 The Autonomous Village and the Development of Chiefdoms. In *Development and Decline: The Evolution of Sociopolitical Organizations*, edited by Henri J. M. Claessen, Pieter van de Velde, and M. Estellie Smith, pp. 141–155. Bergin and Garvey, South Hadley, Massachusetts.

Trautmann, Thomas R.

1997 *Aryans and British India*. University of California Press, Berkeley.

Trigger, Bruce

1989 *A History of Archaeological Thought*. Cambridge University Press, Cambridge.

Tsai, Howard I.

2012a *An Archaeological Investigation of Ethnicity at Las Varas, Peru*. PhD dissertation, University of Michigan, Ann Arbor. University Microfilms, Ann Arbor.

2012b Adobe Bricks and Labor Organization on the North Coast of Peru. *Andean Past* 10:131–167.

2019 The "Coastal Cajamarca" Style Did Not Come from the Coast. *Ñawpa Pacha* 39(1):121–144.

Tschauner, Hartmut

2001 *Socioeconomic and Political Organization in the Late Prehispanic Lambayeque Sphere, Northern North Coast of Peru*. PhD dissertation, Harvard University, Cambridge. University Microfilms, Ann Arbor.

Tschopik, Harry, Jr.

1950 An Andean Ceramic Tradition in Historical Perspective. *American Antiquity* 15(3):196–218.

Tsurumi, Eisei, Evelyn Anyanett Mora Coronado, and Yasutake Kato

2004 Proyecto arqueológico: Las Huacas, valle medio de Jequetepeque, Provincia de

Contumazá, Departamento de Cajamarca. Preliminary report submitted to the Instituto Nacional de Cultura, Lima. Copies available from the Instituto Nacional de Cultura, Cajamarca.

Urton, Gary

1992 Communalism and Differentiation in an Andean Community. In *Andean Cosmologies Through Time: Persistence and Emergence*, edited by Robert V. H. Dover, Katherine E. Seibold, and John H. McDowell, pp. 231–266. Indiana University Press, Bloomington.

Vandemoortele, Kathleen

2011 Late La Tene Oppida in West and Central Europe. PhD dissertation, Cardiff University.

Vargas Ugarte, Rubén

1936 La fecha de la fundación de Trujillo. *Revista Histórica* 10(2):229–239.

Vaughn, Kevin J.

2009 *The Ancient Andean Village: Marcaya in Prehispanic Nasca*. University of Arizona Press, Tucson.

Veit, Ulrich

1994 Ethnic Concepts in German Prehistory: A Case Study on the Relationship between Cultural Identity and Archaeological Objectivity. In *Archaeological Approaches to Cultural Identity*, edited by Stephen Shennan, pp. 35–56. Routledge, London.

Verano, John W.

1986 A Mass Burial of Mutilated Individuals at Pacatnamu. In *The Pacatnamu Papers*, edited by Christopher B. Donnan and Guillermo A. Cock, pp. 117–138. Vol. 1. Museum of Cultural History, University of California, Los Angeles.

2003 Human Skeletal Remains from Machu Picchu: A Reexamination of the Yale Peabody Museum's Collections. In *The 1912 Yale Peruvian Scientific Expedition Collections from Machu Picchu: Human and Animal Remains*, edited by Richard L. Burger and Lucy C. Salazar, pp. 65–117. Yale University Publications in Anthropology No. 85. Department of Anthropology, Yale University, New Haven.

Verano, John W., and Michael J. Deniro

1993 Locals or Foreigners? Morphological, Biometric, and Isotopic Approaches to the Question of Group Affinity in Human Skeletal Remains Recovered from Unusual Archaeological Contexts. In *Investigations of Ancient Human Tissue: Chemical Analyses in Anthropology*, edited by Mary K. Sandford, pp. 361–386. Gordon and Breach, Langhorne, Pennsylvania.

von Neumann, John, and Oskar Morgenstern

1944 *Theory of Games and Economic Behavior*. Princeton University Press, Princeton.

Vos, Jeroen

2006 *Pirámides de agua: Construcción e impacto de imperios de riego en la costa norte del Perú*. Instituto de Estudios Peruanos, Lima.

Wallace, Anthony F. C.

1966 *Religion: An Anthropological View*. Random House, New York.

Wassén, Henry S.
1987 "Ulluchu" in Moche Iconography and Blood Ceremonies: The Search for Identification. *Årstryck, Göteborgs Etnografiska Museum 1985–1986*:59–85.
Watanabe, Shinya
2001 Wari y Cajamarca. In *Huari y Tiwanaku: Modelos vs. Evidencias. Segunda Parte*, edited by Peter Kaulicke and William H. Isbell, pp. 531–541. Boletín de Arqueología PUCP No. 5. Fondo Editorial de la Pontificia Universidad Católica del Perú, Lima.
2002 El reino de Cuismancu: Orígenes y transformación en el Tawantinsuyu. In *Identidad y transformación en el Tawantinsuyu y en los Andes coloniales: Perspectivas arqueológicas y etnohistóricas; Primera parte*, edited by Peter Kaulicke, Gary Urton, and Ian Farrington, pp. 107–136. Boletín de Arqueología PUCP No. 6. Fondo Editorial de la Pontificia Universidad Católica del Perú, Lima.
2006 Una aproximación a la Cultura Cajamarca: Su relación con otras culturas. *Espiga. II Etapa* 9:83–96.
2009 La cerámica caolín en la cultura Cajamarca (sierra norte del Perú): El caso de la fase Cajamarca Media. *Bulletin de l'Institut Français d'Études Andines* 38(2): 205–236.
2015 *Dominio provincial en el Imperio inca*. Shumpusha, Yokohama.
Whiteley, Peter M.
2008 *The Orayvi Split: A Hopi Transformation*. Anthropological Papers No. 87. American Museum of Natural History, New York.
Williams, Patrick Ryan
2001 Cerro Baúl: A Wari Center on the Tiwanaku Frontier. *Latin American Antiquity* 12(1):67–83.
2002 Rethinking Disaster-Induced Collapse in the Demise of the Andean Highland States: Wari and Tiwanaku. *World Archaeology* 33(3):361–374.
Williams, Patrick Ryan, and Donna J. Nash
2006 Sighting the Apu: A GIS Analysis of Wari Imperialism and the Worship of Mountain Peaks. *World Archaeology* 38(3):455–468.
2016 Religious Ritual and Wari State Expansion. In *Ritual and Archaic States*, edited by Joanne M. A. Murphy. University Press of Florida, Gainesville.
Wilson, David J.
1981 Of Maize and Men: A Critique of the Maritime Hypothesis of State Origins on the Coast of Peru. *American Anthropologist* 83(1):93–120.
1988 *Prehispanic Settlement Patterns in the Lower Santa Valley, Peru: A Regional Perspective on the Origins and Development of Complex North Coast Society*. Smithsonian Institution Press, Washington, DC.
1999 *Indigenous South Americans of the Past and Present: An Ecological Perspective*. Westview Press, Boulder, Colorado.
Zapata Rodríguez, Julinho
1997 Arquitectura y contextos funerarios wari en Batan Urqu, Cuzco. In *La muerte en el antiguo Perú*, edited by Peter Kaulicke, pp. 165–206. Boletín de Arqueología PUCP No. 1. Fondo Editorial de la Pontificia Universidad Católica del Perú, Lima.

Index

Page numbers in italics refer to figures and tables.